Praise for *Building a Customer Service Culture:*

Breezy volumes with general customer service advice are a dime a dozen. What is lacking is a real-world guide that everyone in an organization can use to improve customer service inside and outside the organization. Dr. Martinez and Bob Hobbi have finally provided us with a terrific guide.

—*Ralph Vasami, President and CEO,*
Universal Weather and Aviation, Inc.

The success of my organization depends on the "substance and style" of customer service as well as the "why and how" of it. This book provides it all. As a bonus, every reader, from CEO to employee, will take a journey that results in a true passion to help build a genuine customer service culture.

—*Michael R. Cunningham, PhD,*
Chief Executive Officer, Diversified Global Graphics Group

Building a Customer Service Culture is a timely book for the many firms seeking to leverage their distinctive relationships with customers for competitive advantage. Martinez and Hobbi have bundled lots of great content with insightful examples, useful exercises and dependable frameworks to aid managers charged with designing and executing a winning customer service strategy for their companies.

—*Stephen W. Brown, PhD,*
Edward M. Carson Chair in Services Marketing,
Center for Services Leadership Arizona State University

In today's global marketplace, customer service is the difference in gaining and maintaining competitive advantage. That is true for every type of organization—including mine. The authors break down this critical concept of customer service and take the extra step of providing a practical roadmap to create and sustain a culture of service and success for the long term.

—*Gerardo E. de los Santos, President and CEO,*
League for Innovation in the Community College

By reading *Building A Customer Service Culture*, you and your company will improve customer service and view it in a new way; and you will become an active participant in the ever changing dynamic of customer service.

—*Troy Mitchum,*
Director of Front Services Wynn, Las Vegas

More Praise for *Building a Customer Service Culture:*

No matter who your customer and regardless of your business, you need a plan and a process to deliver and inspire outstanding customer service. Martinez and Hobbi have provided us with an outstanding, readily adoptable and user-friendly roadmap. This book is a must have to create and sustain a focused customer service employee culture.

—*Keith R. Sawyer, General Manager,
Chevron Global Aviation*

My company has to create a culture of top-notch service, because the clients we serve have the means and contacts to buy anything, anywhere, anytime. *Building A Customer Service Culture* is the guide to help me not only maintain but exceed their expectations. Read it!

—*Mark E. Mathews, Assistant Vice President,
Robertson Taylor International Brokers*

Most organizations aspire to duplicate the results of the marketplace darlings of customer service but almost never comprehensively meet the benchmarks. Martinez and Hobbi provide a systematic strategy, a how-to manual of sorts, which simplifies the processes necessary to reach new levels of customer service. In short, this book is the cornerstone to building a strong customer service culture. The exercises the authors offer in this book will serve as tools I can continually use to redefine my customer service efforts.

—*Victor Pesqueira, President,
Duck Press—America's Golf Greeting Card Company*

Embrace the material in *Building a Customer Service Culture*, and expect not only the customer service you provide to improve, but your work output and job satisfaction as well.

—*William Garvey, Editor-in-Chief,
Business & Commercial Aviation*

Building a Customer Service Culture

The Seven ServiceElements of Customer Success

Building a Customer Service Culture

The Seven ServiceElements of Customer Success

by

Mario Martinez
University of Nevada, Las Vegas

and

Bob Hobbi
President of ServiceElements

Information Age Publishing, Inc.
Charlotte, North Carolina • www.infoagepub.com

Library of Congress Cataloging-in-Publication Data

Martinez, Mario, 1967-
  Building a customer service culture : the seven service elements of customer success / by Mario Martinez, Bob Hobbi.
    p. cm.
  Includes bibliographical references.
  ISBN 978-1-59311-935-5 (pbk.) -- ISBN 978-1-59311-936-2 (hardcover) 1. Customer services. 2. Customer services--Management. I. Hobbi, Bob. II. Title.
  HF5415.5.M1714 2008
  658.8'12--dc22

                                                                          2008020808

Copyright © 2008 IAP–Information Age Publishing, Inc.

All rights reserved. No part of this publication may be reproduced, stored in a retrieval system, or transmitted in any form or by any electronic or mechanical means, or by photocopying, microfilming, recording, or otherwise without written permission from the publisher.

Printed in the United States of America

To the many customers, family members, and friends who helped us understand what a joy it is to serve others—in business and in life.

CONTENTS

Preface	*xi*
Acknowledgments	*xvii*
1. Defining Customer Service	*1*
2. Profiling the External Customer	*15*
3. From the Inside Out: Internal Customers	*35*
4. Moving Beyond Sameness	*57*
5. Make Time Count, Don't Count Time	*77*
6. Cycle of Services Thinking	*99*
7. Beyond Customer Expectations	*113*
8. Putting it All Together	*129*
About the Authors	*143*

PREFACE

In working with thousands of clients, from small businesses to Fortune 500 companies, we have found that customer service remains more important today than ever before. A plethora of books and experts admonish leaders to support customer service, embrace it from the "top down" or assign an executive responsibility for customer service. This general advice is truly on target, but alone it is insufficient to build a customer service culture. The challenges of providing excellent customer service are formidable. The first challenge before business is that individuals, groups, divisions, and entire companies define customer service very differently. The second and more serious challenge is that a lot of businesses think they know what customer service is and they think they are doing a good job of providing it. As we help people dig below the surface, though, they discover that customer service is more than just a fashionable sounding term that everyone has to use to be competitive. Perhaps more importantly, as people begin to understand the many dimensions of customer service, they are often dismayed to discover that their initial perceptions of how well they deliver customer service does not match the perception of those they are serving. As individuals and companies, we tend to give ourselves much credit when we are asked how well we are doing something, but then when we get down to the details, we find many surprises. This tendency holds for customer service delivery as well.

Customer service is a culture. A culture takes time to build, and tools are needed if one is to build that culture. A customer service culture cannot be taught in a 1-day seminar. Action must accompany the concepts that most books, seminars, and speakers promote. Speakers can talk about customer loyalty, or the latest book on customer service can promote "having a passion" for customer service. This is all good advice, but too general to be useful. Without the tools to help companies and the people who work within them implement that advice, we are left with a feel good fad that begins to fade after a few weeks.

Building a Customer Service Culture: The Seven Service Elements of Customer Success is built upon concepts and tools that lead to action. Indeed, we must get to know our customers better, but the question is how do we actually do that? In this book, you will find many tools and exercises that will help you with the "How do I do it?" The tools and exercises are the result of decades of experience, built on our work with thousands of our own customers who have implemented the ideas contained herein. Our customers are the very people who are in the business of delivering customer service—they are at the front line, leading, managing, and working to make customer service an actual competitive advantage for their companies. We have learned from our customers, and they have learned from us, and the result is what you find in the pages that follow.

Our own experience is also woven into the concepts and tools that you will find throughout the book, primarily because we put into practice with our own customers the very ideas we promote. Finally, experience is the great teacher, but one must also account for the work of others and what they have learned in their studies and practices. Therefore, the final leg upon which this book is built is the research and those others who have preceded us. Without these forerunners and their contributions, we would be unable to grow the field of customer service.

The combination of our own experience, the practice of our customers, and the integration of existing ideas creates a compelling and comprehensive view of customer service that is missing from the many volumes on the topic. In addition, customer service is an evolving field. New considerations emerge almost daily. Many observers thought technology, for example, was going to solve all of our customer service problems. Technology brings with it the chance for automation and individualization, and there are many powerful customer service advantages that have come on the scene as a result. Now, Amazon.com can provide you with recommendations about books that might be of interest to you, based on your pending or previous purchases. Google.com has the capability of customizing advertisements to your interests, as advertisements are matched to the parameters of the very thing you are searching for on the Internet. On the other hand, technology has also created some very real service challenges. Very few people enjoy the experience of automated phone menus, whereby you must go through five or six levels before you can have a chance at talking to a live person. The complexities of technological gadgets also mean that when something breaks or goes wrong, it is unlikely that you can solve the problem yourself. You must now rely on specialists to fix your problems, which can cause untimely and prolonged delays. When you turn to these specialists for help, you expect good customer service.

Social, political, and economic trends are also changing our world—and with it the expectations of our customers. Experienced Babyboomers now mentor Generation Xers, while trying to create products and services for the demographic group now known as Millennials (the 80 million or so people born between 1980 and 1995). Soon, the Millennials will be trying to mentor the next generation. And so it goes.

Different people will continue to work together and interact, for business and pleasure, and demographic and social trends will continue to influence how people interact within an organization and how they serve customers. Adding to the demographic and social complexities is an escalating customer expectation of having anything at anytime. Organizations must be prepared to deliver service in person or to remote customers, to every corner of the globe. And customers are infinitely diverse. You may be delivering service to the CEO of a company or a commanding 5 year old who likes his pizza just so. Whatever service you are providing, we do know that excellence counts—it counts for the customer and it counts on your bottom line. Customers are more willing than ever to spend money for quality, customization, and service. Those companies that pay attention to the details of how to meet the foundational human needs of their customers, which is at the core of providing a great customer experience, will experience both soulful and financial growth for their employees and organizations.

With all the changes occurring around us, definitive formulas and generic advice are no longer useful in helping you or your organization reach new levels of customer service. You must be involved in the process of learning useful concepts and then applying them to your unique environment. Customers are different, and so are the people who provide the service. The mélange of personalities, needs, preferences, and interactions is incredibly complex and varied, spurring the need for application tools that can be customized to every person giving and receiving service.

The answer to building a customer service culture is to apply concepts and tools around the seven ServiceElements found in this book. Chapter 1 explains the first ServiceElement, which is defining customer service. We must have a broad understanding of what we mean by customer service as a starting point. You will reconcile some of your own experiences with some typical notions of customer service. Then, in chapters 2 and 3, you will find the second and third ServiceElements. You will study external and internal customers, and apply new knowledge and your own knowledge in ways that help you customize the service you deliver to each. Most of us automatically think of people who buy our products or services (external customers) when we think of customer service, but chapter 3 takes special care to emphasize how our work relationships with our colleagues ultimately influences the level of service we provide to outside customers. The fourth ServiceElement, in chapter 4, urges us to look at the attributes of our own product or service. What is so special about it—in your eyes and the customers' eyes? The secret element here is finding something that moves us beyond being like everyone else. In addition, the key to providing a sustainable and ongoing customer experience for internal and external customers is only possible when you are able to master your own activities. Chapter 5 provides you with some tools that move beyond traditional time management so that you can master your activity and thus consistently deliver excellent service. The sixth ServiceElement requires you to take a fundamental yet simple look at your activities and processes through the lens of the customer. What steps in your activities and processes are most likely endearing customers versus driving them away? The tools in this chapter will help you find important leverage points. In chapter 7, we will provide you with some information on the different types of customers and help you think about the types of customers that you have. Currently, there are several books that encourage us to move beyond customer satisfaction, or to create loyalty. The basis of all of this, however, is to understand how customer expectations and satisfaction work to produce different types of customers. Finally, in chapter 8, we provide the three ingredients that you need in order to truly and effectively implement all seven ServiceElements.

Serving others effectively is an ongoing effort; it is not a destination but a journey. Our world and the people who populate it are in constant flux, and so our assumptions about what we do and how we do it need constant reexamination. *Building a Customer Service Culture: The Seven ServiceElements of Customer Success* is the guide that will help you create a customized plan to embark on the greatest activity of all: serving others.

Mario Martinez
Bob Hobbi
August 2008

ACKNOWLEDGMENTS

Customer service is and will continue to be a differentiator for successful organizations and successful people. It is to that end that we wish to acknowledge just a few of the many groups and individuals who provided us with the type of customer service that made our book possible. A very special thanks goes to the many companies and people within the business and general aviation industry who shared with us and contributed to the ongoing development of our own ideas. This industry has some of the most demanding and discerning customers in the business world, and much of what we learned came through industry experts and the very customers they serve.

We also wish to thank George Johnson, from Information Age Publishing. George and his team have been easy to work with and encouraged us of the merits of our project, from the very beginning. Ashley Parkhurst has a true talent for writing and editing in the English language; and she read, reread, and edited every page of this book. We are thankful to Ashley because of her willingness to give the manuscript attention when we needed it the most. Farshad K. Adam, from 8Graphics, did a wonderful job on the graphics and book design. Finally, we thank the many colleagues who were willing to read the manuscript and provide feedback—for it is that feedback that provided the encouragement to improve and move forward with our project.

CHAPTER 1

DEFINING CUSTOMER SERVICE

INTRODUCTION

Customer service has been a formal cornerstone of competitiveness for well over 30 years. The tenets of excellent customer service are central to the success of private business, government agencies, education institutions, or any organization that creates or delivers products or services. Customer service is as important for emerging businesses in Asia as it is for mature industries in Europe and America. Customer service is critical for sales divisions as well as internal functional departments. Though the nuances of how customer service may be delivered across international borders may vary, the foundational principles and ideas that underlie excellent service remain.

There is a problem, however. Organizations and the people who work within them have difficulty implementing the principles of customer service. The vast majority of books and training materials on customer service teach general concepts but do not provide the tools to implement them. Knowing is different from doing; and doing requires more than just having the "head knowledge" of a good idea. Doing requires that you have the tools to help you implement the principles of customer service and bring them to life on a daily basis. Without the tools, we intuitively know what must be done to deliver excellent customer service, but we have difficulty practicing it. Common sense is often not common practice in customer service because there is a scarcity of tools to allow for this implementation. The key to providing good tools is very simple: you must have the opportunity to answer questions and do exercises that draw on your own experiences and apply to your situations. It is easier to internalize the ideas of excellent customer service when we draw on our own experiences as opposed to just reading about the concepts or theories. Customer service is in many respects an art form, which is fluid and ever changing.

In *Building a Customer Service Culture*, we take you on an enjoyable journey where you will learn about the foundational principles of customer service and acquire the tools to implement those principles. Some of the principles and concepts are part of the collective wisdom of what we already know about customer service. Other principles will be new, especially because they are combined with questions and exercises that draw on research to help you improve how you think about and deliver customer service. In the pages that follow, we draw on the latest research from such fields as psychology, organizational behavior and business strategy to create new insights about how to make customer service a sustainable competitive advantage in your job and for your organization.

On this journey, you will discover that customer service is both an individual and organizational commitment. We all have different strengths that help us deliver excellent customer service, and that is where our uniqueness can flourish. At the same time, no person is an island. The contributions we willingly make to our organizations create a collective strength that individuals working toward selfish ends cannot achieve alone. It is the collection of individual efforts that, when added together, create a true customer service culture and make life and work more fun.

Interestingly enough, the accomplishment that each team member feels when he or she has delivered excellent customer service most powerfully makes its presence with the feedback that a satisfied customer provides. This person-to-person feedback remains the number one source of job satisfaction for every team member who has experienced it. This feedback can come from a customer who has just bought your product or service or a coworker with whom you teamed to complete a significant project. Of course, there are also the real results associated with excellent customer service. The results for a private business may show up as an increase in net profits while the local soup kitchen's accomplishment is that everyone who came for a meal was well fed.

Perhaps the most important contribution of *Building a Customer Service Culture* is that it is really a book about finding meaning in your job and creating satisfaction for others in whatever it is that you do. In this sense, you will find that the information is as much about making you a more effective and satisfied team member as it is about delivering world-class customer service. The place to start this journey is with the big picture, by defining what we mean by customer service. This is the first ServiceElement, and it begins our quest to deliver excellent customer service and create a culture that sustains it.

Defining Customer Service

Though many of us know it when we receive it, good customer service is sometimes difficult to define. Organizations deliver different products and services, and the modes of service delivery vary by person. Yet, there are some common characteristics that define good customer service. Many books describe customer service, but the explanations are abstract and difficult to internalize. Readers are too often left with the question: How does this relate to me and my job—the things that I do on a daily basis? Frequently, there are no applications or exercises to give us the opportunity to draw on our own experiences, or to help us really create a picture of what we really mean by customer service.

Good explanations, definitions, and actions are best achieved by going from the general to the specific. In this way, a good first step to define customer service is to think of some organizations that we generally associate with excellent customer service. Then, we can begin to narrow down the characteristics that make those organizations great examples of customer service excellence. Finally, to get to the specific, you must draw on your personal experiences and then see if there are connections between what you and others define as excellent customer service.

As a first step, think of three organizations that you equate with excellent customer service. You may even have such specific experience with the organization that

Exercise 1

Three Organizations that Deliver Excellent Customer Service

1. _____

    a. _____

    b. _____

2. _____

    a. _____

    b. _____

3. _____

    a. _____

    b. _____

---

you name a particular department within the organization that you are thinking about. Write down those three organizations in the spaces numbered 1, 2, and 3 in Exercise 1. In spaces a. and b. in Exercise 1, write down two short descriptions of why you think these organizations deliver excellent customer service.

People who attend customer service training seminars and workshops commonly mention companies like Starbucks, Disney, Southwest Airlines, and Enterprise Rent-A-Car. You are probably familiar with these three companies, and you may have even listed some of them in Exercise 1. Here are additional examples that are commonly mentioned as top customer service companies:

- Barnes and Noble Bookstores
- Williams-Sonoma
- Singapore Airlines

What is it that makes these organizations so good at delivering excellent customer service? In Exercise 1, you created two explanations of why you think the organizations you listed exemplify excellent customer service. Let's describe some of the things that model organizations do to create new customers and establish loyalty among existing ones by delivering top-notch customer service.

Starbucks offers a comfortable atmosphere—a home away from home—and knowledgeable baristas who will customize your drink (special orders don't upset them, in fact they are welcomed); Disney offers a magical experience that is known throughout the globe; Southwest Airlines has low prices, crew members who have a great sense of humor, and point-to-point service to numerous destinations; Enterprise hires college graduates who dress professionally and treat every customer as a VIP (Very Important Person), they provide a complimentary bottle of water to weary travelers, and they have no problem picking up a customer from a proximate destination; Barnes and Noble offers a helpful staff, brick and mortar stores as well as online options, and extensive children's selections along with the normal topical book sections one would expect; Williams-Sonoma offers upscale cooking products and foods, with a knowledgeable staff that exudes the quality that one finds in the products; Singapore Airlines since its inception in 1972 continues to post quarterly profits, with its first-class passengers dining on everything from exquisite seafood to finest steak, while all passengers enjoy the pampered treatment that the flight attendants (commonly known as the "Singapore Girls") deliver to passengers who at any time may be choosing from a host of movies or games while reclining their seats into beds; and Jiffy Lube delivers fast oil changes at reasonable prices, and keeps maintenance records for your automobile while providing some of those maintenance services that it may need.

These are all the things that these excellent organizations provide or do, but the question still remains: Why is it that we feel that they provide excellent customer service? After all, can't any company offer excellent products, fancy meals, or well-trained college graduates? To truly define customer service, you must think about what you personally associate with good or bad customer service. What is it that you have experienced that makes you think a company or an organization—one you listed above or any other one—delivers excellent customer service.

Since we have just discussed exemplary organizations and the things they do, you should now think about the opposite side of the coin: bad customer service. There is much research to suggest that your bad experiences are deeply impressionable. In fact, you are sometimes better able to recall and describe bad experiences more accurately than good ones! Bad experiences are often accompanied by intense emotions, which make them memorable. It may be the pessimistic side of us all, but it is also true that most of us notice the one dirty speck on the windshield and not the other 99% of it that is clean. All of this means that it is extremely important to make sure every customer has a good experience, repeatedly. We can become more sensitive to our customers by going through an exercise that emphasizes what we do not like and therefore what we should try to avoid giving to others who use our products and services.

What are the characteristics you associate with BAD customer service? Think about some absolutely negative experiences you have had when you received terrible customer service. Was it in a store or restaurant? On an airline? At a university or government office? Was it when you were calling a help desk and trying to get some information? Was it when you had trouble navigating through a long, automated phone system and then had to repeat all of your information when you finally reached a live human being? Perhaps you received a bill from the hospital that seemed incorrect, and you visited the billing department, only to leave in total frustration? What did that feel like? How would you describe it?

Exercise 2 is called a free-association exercise. In the middle oval in Exercise 2, you see the words "BAD Customer Service." In addition, there are four ovals surrounding the middle oval. In the four ovals, list four words or phrases that come to your mind when you think about BAD customer service.

Attached to each outside oval in Exercise 2, you will find a connecting line with two blanks. If there are additional words that you are able to associate with one of these outside ovals, or perhaps that helps describe more clearly what you mean by a certain term, then fill in the blanks. For example, you may associate "Indifference" with bad customer service, so you would put the word Indifference in one of the four outside ovals. If you wish to fill in the two blanks, you must think about what

 Exercise 2

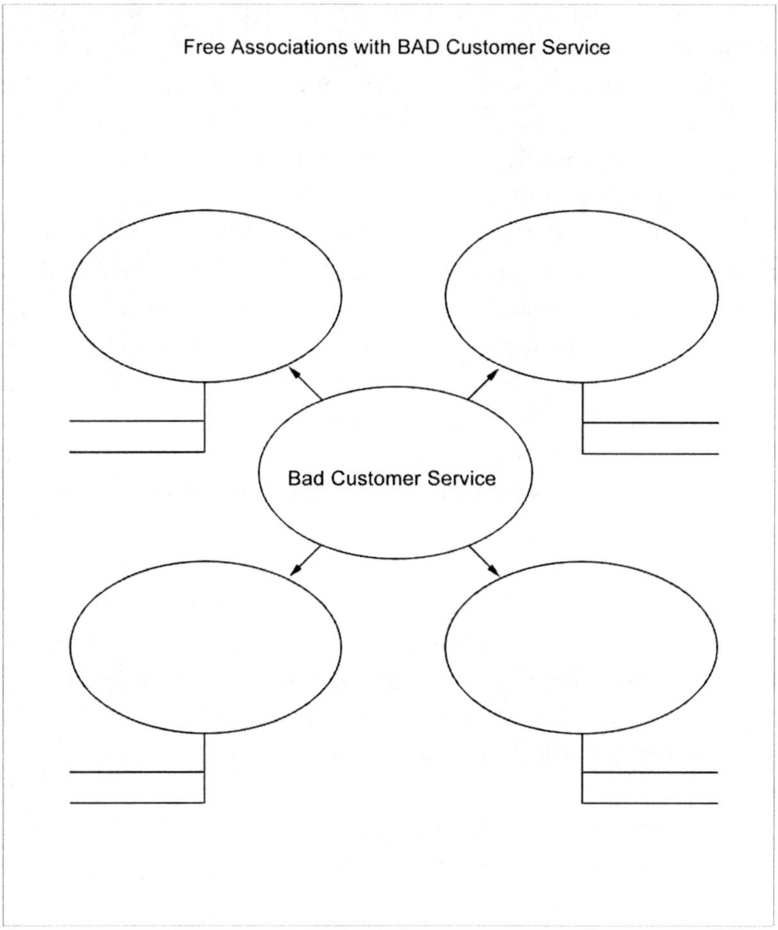

Free Associations with BAD Customer Service

Bad Customer Service

caused you to feel like the company or a person was indifferent when providing the product or service you purchased? Let's say the employee who was helping you made no eye contact and didn't thank you for your business. You might put "No eye contact" and "Didn't convey appreciation" as characteristics that you associate with indifference.

Go through Exercise 2 and simply brainstorm a list of four major attributes (in the ovals) that you personally associate with bad customer service, and then fill out two characteristics (in the blanks) that you believe describe each attribute you wrote down in the ovals. If you are able to recall specific experiences in great detail, you will be able to complete this exercise very quickly.

The free association picture you fashion in Exercise 2 is simply a tool to create a portrait of your personalized definition of bad customer service. This portrait is based on your experiences and your interpretations of the types of service you would rather do without. You have listed things that bother you; things that you do not like when others are delivering service to you. Beware! You must be careful not to make the same mistakes you have seen others commit.

We have conducted Exercise 2 with thousands of people in seminars and workshops in the United States and around the world. Although we ask participants to conduct this exercise alone, some very common attributes of bad customer service repeatedly emerge at every workshop when people compare notes:

Commonly Cited Attributes of Bad Customer Service

- Bad attitude
- Ill-mannered, rude, or unfriendly
- Does not provide answers, makes excuses
- Inconsistency
- Inflexibility
- Poor communication; doesn't keep the customer informed

- Impersonal
- Indifference
- Slow response to questions or requests

Let's take a few examples from the list of Attributes of Bad Customer Service and delve into them a bit more. Consider inconsistent customer service. Inconsistency is an attribute of bad customer service that people usually list as problematic. Why? Inconsistency leads to poor quality and unpredictable customer service. The former company, People Express Airline, serves as a notorious example of inconsistent service. People Express Airline started in 1981 and in 2 years was the fastest growing airline in the country, with its signature low-cost fares and limited service. In 1985, two years after its peak, the airline started to crumble, due to overexpansion, sharp competition, and overwhelmed operations. In short, the company was unable to properly manage its growth, and though customers didn't expect 5-star service, they expected a certain level of quality, customer service, and consistency. It just wasn't there, and People Express Airline was eventually bought out by Continental.

Now, the reason it was necessary for you to fill in the blanks in the free-association exercise is because even if we all associate a particular attribute with bad customer service, the specifics of how we define that attribute may differ. For example, most people believe a bad attitude and inflexibility are attributes of bad customer service. However, our definitions of bad attitude and inflexibility may be vastly different. A California native visiting a fancy French restaurant in Paris may find that the waiter has a bad attitude and seems condescending when everyone at the table orders a round of decaffeinated coffee. Many restaurants in France do not even carry decaffeinated coffee. A New Yorker, who is also in the dining party, may find the waiter's attitude a perfectly acceptable form of direct communication and even somewhat amusing. The New Yorker may believe such forms of communication are normal and should not be taken personally when dining in France.

You may have listed some of the Commonly Cited Attributes of Bad Customer Service in your individualized free-association exercise (Exercise 2). The blank lines that you filled in are the details of how you define bad customer service, given your perceptions, your expectations, and how you want service delivered. Although our interpretations of how we define things like rudeness and inconsistency may vary, there are some common threads that connect every attribute of bad customer service.

First, human relations, or people skills, are important. Organizations and their employees communicate with each other and with their customers. Employees with strong people skills are better able to assess customers and avoid the dangers of projecting such customer service killers as a negative attitude or unfriendliness. Employees with strong people skills are able to pick up cues and thus interpret and read what the customer expects and how the customer best receives and accepts customer service.

Second, and most importantly, it is possible, through training and coaching, to turn every bad attribute into a good attribute that strengthens customer service. Every person, regardless of prior job experience, personal background, or personality can learn how to deliver excellent customer service. This is critical since every person on your team either contributes to or takes away from creating a positive customer service experience," rather than just "customer service." Training, coaching, and education can help anyone improve his or her customer service skills and thereby contribute to a positive customer service culture.

You may already provide top-notch service to your customers, and your company may already have an established, well-deserved reputation for excellent customer service. Still, by completing the exercises throughout the book and utilizing the tools you will find throughout the remaining chapters, you can be assured of improving upon or retaining your top spot. Excellent customer service is common sense, and common sense will continue to be common practice for you.

Along with the exercises and questions throughout the book, we provide information and examples so that you can personally apply the knowledge you gain from reading each chapter. Through this process, you can turn any attribute of bad customer service into an attribute of excellent customer service. It is only through conscious effort that your customers will talk about you and your organization as models of customer service, aptly described by the following:

Commonly Cited Attributes of Excellent Customer Service

- Positive attitude
- Well-mannered, attentive, and friendly
- Provide answers or finds the answers, but doesn't make excuses
- Consistency
- Flexibility
- Sincerity
- Good communication; keeps the customer informed
- Personable
- Quick response to questions or requests

The road to excellent customer service really does start with defining it. All of the attributes in the above list define excellent customer service; conversely, all of the attributes you highlighted in Exercise 2 define bad customer service. In Exercise 2, you also created some details to customize your definition of bad customer service. Defining customer service, both good and bad, is the first of the *Seven ServiceElements of Customer Success*. The next step is to define the customer, the topic of chapter 2.

Service summary for chapter 1

♦ Define excellent customer service by thinking about your own customer service experiences and then describing them;

♦ People will remember bad customer service experiences more clearly than good customer service experiences;

♦ Define bad customer service so you are sensitive to what you wish to avoid doing when you are delivering customer service;

♦ Most attributes of excellent customer service rely on strong people skills;

♦ Any person, who is willing, can learn to deliver excellent customer service.

CHAPTER 2

PROFILING THE EXTERNAL CUSTOMER

All organizations have one thing in common: they depend on customers to stay in business. There are many ways to make customers want, need, and even depend on your products and services, but in order to create this relationship you must understand the customer. Next, you must define and profile the customer. This is the second ServiceElement.

Customers are multidimensional, which means they do not come in standard packages and act the same way. They have different backgrounds, expectations, and experiences. Further complicating the issue is that a customer may be buying the same service from you at two different times for two totally different reasons. Consider a restaurant patron who arrives one day with a group of business associates, but he visits on another day with a group of friends for a social occasion. The two situations are entirely different from this customer's perspective, and so too are his expectations different for each situation. The customer's expectations at the business meal include timeliness and limited presence by the waiter. Expectations for the social meal are more relaxed, and the party of friends may want the waiter to be friendly and talkative. The individuals attending the social outing are probably not as concerned about time as people attending an afternoon lunch break from work.

The endless variables that describe the customer can be overwhelming. That is why the second ServiceElement works to create a definition and profile of the customer. By creating a customer profile, we deepen our understanding of the customer. An accurate customer profile cannot be captured in a single sentence or one pithy definition, for that would not do justice to the real world situations we face with our customers. The profile does not, however, have to be overly complex either. What we need is a foundation for understanding our customers. This foundation should account for the dynamics that underline customer wants, needs, and expectations, yet it should be usable, easy to remember, and easy to communicate across the organization.

A comprehensive approach to profiling our customers can be accurately completed in three steps. As Figure 2.1 shows, the steps consist of asking three simple questions about our customers:

- Who Are They?
- What Do They Want or Need?
- How Have They Changed?

Many organizations leave it up to the marketing department, or perhaps a group of select leaders, to answer these questions. Those organizations that involve all of their employees in thinking about and answering

Figure 2.1

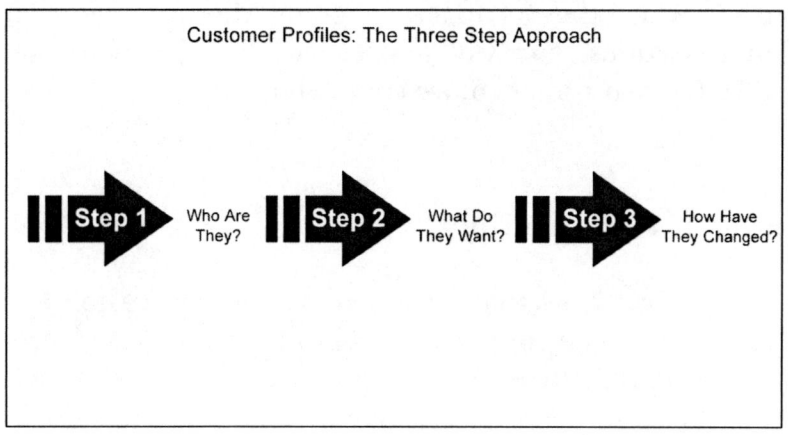

these questions create a competitive advantage for one very compelling reason: they are tapping the knowledge and experience of every employee to help profile the customers. It is often the front line employee who has the most experience and knowledge dealing with the customer directly. For instance, a business analyst who arranges the logistics for product delivery to the customer may never see the customer face-to-face. It may be that the carrier (the person who actually delivers the product) is the one who really knows the customer on a personal level. Still, both the business analyst and the carrier have knowledge and information about the customer, and both are needed to more comprehensively understand her. The key is for the business analyst and carrier to communicate with each other so that they are both fully aware of who this customer is, what it is that she wants and needs, and how she has changed over time.

You know your customers best. If you go through some systematic exercises, you will create a more complete picture of who your customers are and what they want. You will also be able to adjust to their wants and needs when they change. By going through the next three sections, you will answer questions to help you serve your customers more completely.

Step 1: Who Are They?

Let's first draw some distinctions between customers. There are, to be sure, many types of customers that you influence, directly or indirectly, based on your job activities. The customers that first come to mind for most people are those that buy something from us. In other words, the customer is not paid by our company but rather helps our company pay the bills. The customer comes to us from outside the company. Customers that come from outside the company and pay us for our products or services are called External Customers. The following list describes your External Customers. The list is general, but it is the first step that helps us understand this type of customer.

- Any person who buys our products or services
- Any person who is not paid by our organization but interacts with people who do belong to our organization
- Any company or organization that buys our products or services
- Individuals, groups, departments, companies, or organizations who interact with people who do belong to your organization but are not paid by your organization.

An external customer can be an individual, another company, a department, or any group of people who buy from us or interact with us. The above list is general enough that it can be used to describe any organization's external customers. You can make this list specific to your department, organization and job, by asking yourself "Who are my external customers?" Just to get some additional insight, before you actually answer this question for yourself, take a look at the list of the different external customers for four very different organizations in Table 2.1.

Table 2.1 shows the different types of external customers for a business aviation company, a hospital, a credit union, and a hotel and casino. The responses in Table 2.1 are examples that participants in our seminars cited to describe their external customers. The business aviation company provides an interesting example. Many business aviation companies provide personalized flight hours to clients, meaning that the client can buy a certain amount of flight time on a business aircraft. The size of the aircraft can range from the small and simple to the large and luxurious. The people who purchase flight time are among the most demanding customers in the world, ranging from corporate CEOs to musicians and actors. Such customers expect their flights to be timely and safe, and they place such a high value on their own time that they are willing to pay a premium for personalized flight time. Indeed, private aviation customers have extremely high expectations precisely because they pay a large price for the service they receive. In fact, an external customer for a business aviation company might be described as anyone with enough resources to demand more value than they believe they can get on a commercial airliner.

The external customers for the hospital, credit union, and Las Vegas Hotel also demonstrate how valuable it is to define customers in both general and specific terms.

Table 2.1

External Customers for Four Different Organizations

Business Aviation Company	A Metropolitan Hospital	A Local Credit Union	A Las Vegas Hotel and Casino
Individual pilots	Patients	Individuals, Families	Vacationers
CEOs	Insurance Companies	Small businesses	Convention attendees
Business people	Pharmacies	Public employees, such as teachers and government workers	Business travelers
Actors, singers	Expectant Mothers		Visiting family of local population
Wealthy Individuals	Patient's family		International travelers
Whoever can afford to charter a business aircraft	Chaplin, Clergy		

Patients are obviously customers, from the perspective of the hospital. But there are many different kinds of patients. An expectant mother is one type of patient, an elderly man with a heart condition quite another. Children are patients, but so are middle age adults. Furthermore, most patients have family members who are concerned and accompany their loved ones to the hospital. The family interacts with the staff, and they likely share some responsibility for paying for the services their loved one is receiving from the staff. Family members are customers, too.

The credit union might just define customers as individuals who open accounts, but there are joint accounts, minor accounts, business accounts and oftentimes special privileges for customers who are public employees. The benefit of specifying families and small businesses as customers simply reminds us that different customers use services in different ways. Some come for loans, others to establish checking or savings accounts, and still others seek investment advice.

Finally, the Las Vegas Hotel and casino customer profiles in Table 2.1 show a range of customers. Vacationers and conventioneers are important to the Las Vegas Hotel and casino industry, but many establishments in the area have also been quite successful targeting international travelers or friends and relatives of local Las Vegans. Different types of visitors enjoy the glittering lights and nonstop activity of the famous city, and there are usually a host of hotels and casinos that eagerly seek to meet the various entertainment needs of such a diverse customer base.

Now that you have seen examples of who the external customers might be for four different types of organizations, you are ready to answer the question "Who are my external customers?" Complete Exercise 3 by listing at least five of your external customers.

Completion of Exercise 3 leads us to the next step in defining our customers.

Step 2: What Do They Want?

Much has been written in the last 5 years of what customers want. In their excellent book, *Trading Up*, Michael Silverstein and Neil Fiske, rightly point out that customers want quality, and they are willing to pay for

 Exercise 3

List Five External Customers

1. _____

2. _____

3. _____

4. _____

5. _____

it—or trade up. The initial success of eateries such as Panera Bread (freshly made bread, with healthy soups and sandwiches) and Chipotles (quality burritos) proves that customers are willing to pay $8 to $10 for a good, quality lunch instead of $4 or $5 dollars for unhealthy fast food. There is a Chipotles restaurant near the heart of the financial district in New York City. At lunch time, this restaurant serves hundreds of customers, all searching for a quick, healthy lunch. Customers come by the droves to buy Chipolte's, even though it costs substantially more than a hotdog from the local vendor on the corner. American Girl dolls are priced in the neighborhood of $100, but we parents have been buying them by the masses. We want our daughters to have wholesome dolls that look like actual little girls and not swimsuit models. Not only do we purchase the high-priced dolls, but we also pay top dollar for American Girl doll clothes, brushes, and handbags. The American Girl store in New York City sells an assortment of these accessories, all at a substantial price, along with various services such as hair styling for your daughter's beloved doll. Bread, burritos, or dolls can fetch a high price if customers perceive quality, because quality is what they want and what they are willing to pay for.

How can companies provide the products and services at a level of quality that meets what customers want? In what can only be described as a profound insight, Silverstein and Fiske articulate a ladder of benefits that competitive companies provide: technical, functional, and emotional. Technical benefits account for differences in design, features, or materials; functional benefits account for differences in how the product performs; and finally, emotional benefits account for differences in how the product or service engages the customer on an emotional level.

American Girl dolls are designed with fine materials, such as real buttons and wigged hair, and because of these technical benefits, there is a price premium. Each doll also comes with a unique American history. When the individuality of the doll is combined with the technical benefits, we have a product that has functional benefits for its young consumers because of its characteristics and perceived uniqueness. And since most young girls want to have friends and are drawn to the wholesome look and description of the dolls, the dolls connect with their young customers on an emotional level. American Girl dolls are as much about selling stories and values as they are about selling products. Clearly, products or services that provide all three benefits have the best chance at being successful. When you purchase an American Girl doll for your child, you are buying both a product and a service, perhaps even an experience for your child.

In *The Experience Economy*, Joseph Pines and James Gilmore provide irrefutable evidence of how important it is to provide an experience for the customer. For many people, companies like Starbucks, Harley Davidson, and WholeFoods produce a product(s) and deliver a service(s), but they do so much more. They provide an experience, or they convince the customer that they are providing an experience. Starbucks provides quality coffee in a home-away-from-home atmosphere. The product is good and the venue welcomes even the most discriminating customer. Harley Davidson manufactures some of the best motorcycles on the planet. Not only that, but it encourages middle-aged adults and the Babyboom generation to put on leather chaps, ride with the wind, and look "tough" while walking around a small town during a gas stop. That is an experience indeed, and one that many of Harley's customers desire (at a conscious or unconscious level) and can actually fulfill by riding a Harley.

WholeFoods Supermarkets has made shopping for groceries a fun adventure. You can visit a WholeFoods and eat a fine lunch at a number of specialty areas, which may include sushi or sundry meats and cheeses. When you walk down the butcher's aisle, a friendly worker cries out to offer a sumptuous sample of organic brisket topped with succulent barbeque sauce. For the novice shopper, products are clearly marked so that it is clear what is 100% organic and what meets the WholeFoods standards of quality. At WholeFoods, you may bump into an environmentalist, a corporate executive, or a stay-at-home mom. All are looking for healthy food but each finds so much more. Shopping at WholeFoods is a truly engaging, high value, fun experience—and usually a pretty expensive one, too.

This analysis of experiences, products and services, you may say, has gone too far. Maybe all that people really want is a quality product or service, and they are willing to pay for that quality. This is undoubtedly true, yet the quality of a product or service, and our consumption of it, is intricately tied to the experience of that consumption. Our experience is tied to our feelings, or the emotional connection that is established as a result of the consumption of a product or receipt of a service. Tony Buzman, in his book, *The Mind Map Book*, shows that our brains make pathways and connections that touch on an emotional and logical level when we experience something with our senses. Those connections are also made when we consume a product or receive excellent customer service. If, for example, you receive excellent customer service when renting a car, flying on an airplane or staying at a hotel, it is impossible to avoid the emotional experiences that the brain automatically creates as a result of receiving that service. The brain produces an imprint of that experience, whether we want it to or not. That imprint will influence your future decisions about what you wish to experience or consume.

So, what does this all mean? What does the customer really want? Pines and Gilmore are right: the customer wants an experience. Savvy customers seek out and expect an experience for their money. What many people overlook is that not all customers who buy from us consciously seek a specific experience, understand they are having an experience (good or bad), or realize that this experience influences whether they will buy from us again. Silverstein and Fiske are also right, though, because customers want technical, functional and emotional benefits. The greater these benefits, the deeper and more influential is the experience.

The final word on what customers want requires you to put yourself in the role of the customer. As customers, most of us want to be recognized as individuals who are unique and special. Products and services that allow us to combine different benefits in different ways create unique thoughts, feelings, and emotions. It does not matter whether we are riding motorcycles or talking to a customer service representative trying to demystify a vexing computer problem, we are all after a quality experience that provides some sort of benefit or solution to a problem. Customers want quality, benefits, and solutions to their problems. That is what you want when you are the customer, and that is what every one of your customers wants as well.

Step 3: How Have They Changed?

Janet is an avid reader and loves Jane Austin books. She also collects movies that are based on the books. The "Hollywood" version of *Pride and Prejudice* recently was released on DVD, but Janet was eager to buy the 1996 version of the movie as well so that she could compare the two. Janet went to a local store and found that the two-disk 1996 version was $39.99. Unwilling to pay the $39.99 price tag, Janet went home and searched for vendors online. She eventually found a copy of the 1996 DVD for $17.99 plus a $3.50 shipping charge and ordered the movie. Janet's experience with online shopping is just a single example of a broader trend: consumers have access to more real-time information to compare products, prices, and features than ever before. With more information, customers increasingly expect more, from personalized solutions to instantaneous service.

Technology and the Internet have given potential customers access to information that previously took weeks to obtain or, worse, was unavailable. Now, with a click of a button, comparable information is immediately available. It used to be that a car shopper was considered savvy if he could find the invoice price of a particular vehicle and had different payment scenarios figured out prior to making an offer. Today, all of this information is incredibly easy to obtain. If you are buying a used vehicle, many dealerships even offer to show you a fax of the car's history, the Blue Book value, and anything else you wish to know. The dealerships offer this information (sometimes only when asked) because they know that the customer can also obtain it. Loyalty is built more quickly by being honest and up-front, especially if you know the customer can obtain information that you may be hiding.

More information is not necessarily a good thing. Suddenly, every customer becomes an expert. Consider the experience of one pilot who provides flight service for Fortune 500 clients. "Resourceful business people browse the web just like everyone else, and so they may look at different types of aircraft, weather reports, and technical information related to aviation," he says. "Now, all of a sudden, some of my passengers are the experts on how fast we should be able to get to a destination and what kind of weather systems we should be able to travel through; and they argue with our flight attendants and let them know their opinions." According to this pilot, a little too much information is dangerous in the customer's hands. It causes stress for the flight attendants and leads to complaints when the customer is deplaning. Customer service takes on a whole new dimension in these situations, because now you have to manage a relationship with someone who thinks they have your level of expertise but most likely does not. Customer management becomes a critical service skill in these instances.

Whether your customers' perceptions are right or wrong—even if they are based on a misinterpretation of information—they will look for alternatives if you do not manage these perceptions properly. Customers are able to access different options since technology makes information on alternatives easily accessible. This has changed customers. We must assume that they are more informed, savvy, and easily able to compare competitors. If they are not more informed, most of them believe they are, because they have done a little browsing on the web. As a result, customers may have developed misperceptions which must be delicately managed.

Good customer service and proactive customer management build loyalty. Today, loyalty must be earned because, as economists say, switching costs are low. A customer can easily switch from one product or service to another without much cost to himself, either monetarily or psychologically. There are many choices, substitutes, and alternatives, and people today are more willing than ever to experiment with new and different things.

Customers have more information than ever before and they expect you to earn their loyalty, but that is not the only change that has happened. Malcolm Gladwell, in his book, *Blink*, tells why Bob Golomb, the director of sales at Flemington Nissan Dealership, in Flemington, New Jersey, treats every person who walks into his dealership as a very important person. Every person, no matter who they are, how they look, or how they are dressed, is a potential customer and should receive the best service possible. It does not matter if the person entering the dealership is a 30-something male or a 17-year-old teenage girl. Golomb has learned to provide as much attention and service to the 17-year-old as the 30-something yuppie. It has happened too many times that the teenager shops around only to arrive later that day with her mother and father, who are ready to make a purchase for their daughter.

The customers who use five star hotels and business aviation services have also changed. Companies in these markets no longer serve corporate CEOs and top business people exclusively. Customers in these industries can include rock and rap stars, professional athletes, or children of high-income parents who are taking a trip to meet friends. Many of these customers do not arrive in slacks and a tie, but instead they are wearing jeans and sneakers, and they show up with a friend or two. The CEO and business market is still strong, it is just that five star hotels and business aviation employees now have to be prepared to deliver service and experience to a broader range of customers, who have different needs and varying expectations.

Have your customers' needs, wants, and preferences changed over the years? Look at the list of five customers you created at the beginning of the chapter. Is your list comprised of people who have different lifestyles or income levels? Is there a difference in age among your customers? Do they come from different areas of the country or even the globe? Do they have access to technology? Are you now selling to entire businesses (business to business) instead of to individuals? If you answered yes to any of these questions, then it is almost guaranteed that your customers have changed—and they may be changing again, just when you get used to adjusting your service to their needs!

DELIVERING EXCELLENT EXTERNAL CUSTOMER SERVICE

If you know who your customers are, what they want, and how they have changed, you have answered the necessary questions to build an accurate customer profile. The last remaining question is, given all of this information, "How can I deliver excellent customer service, the type of service my customers are expecting?" The answer to this question is provided in the list of commonly cited attributes of excellent customer service, from chapter 1. The list is worth repeating and is shown below for easy reference.

Commonly Cited Attributes of Excellent Customer Service

- Positive attitude
- Well-mannered, attentive, and friendly
- Provide answers or finds the answers, but doesn't make excuses
- Consistency
- Flexibility
- Sincerity
- Good communication; keeps the customer informed
- Personable
- Quick response to questions or requests

All of the attributes of excellent customer service necessarily involve some form of communication and interaction. This communication and interaction may be face-to-face, over the telephone, or in writing via e-mail or regular mail. Excellent external customer service depends on the same attributes we used to describe excellent companies and excellent customer service. Your success in delivering a service that makes the customer want to come back depends on your ability to connect with the customer on a very personal level.

The value of profiling customers (Who are they? What they want? How they have changed?) is that it generates information and knowledge about our customers. The more knowledge we have of the customer, the better we are able to adjust to the needs and wants of the customer, given his or her unique background and expectations. And though the attributes of excellent customer service are the same for virtually every situation, the way in which those attributes are delivered to and interpreted by the customer often vary. For example, customers seek friendly and well-mannered communication. We have seen, though, that the group of business associates who are out for a working lunch may wish to have only short, friendly communication with their waiter or waitress, whereas the group of casual diners may enjoy more informal interaction with their host.

Excellent customer service, then, requires a conscious effort and a certain kind of intelligence. People who deliver excellent customer service must have the social skills to practice the commonly cited attributes of excellent service. The implementation of such attributes as good communication and friendliness, however, requires someone who understands the customer and knows how to read social situations and quickly respond in an appropriate manner. It is the reading of and responding to the situation that presents a customer service challenge for many people and organizations. Customers always give us clues, in the things that they say and do, which indicate how we should deliver their service.

No matter how we slice it, if you are to deliver excellent customer service, you must know about your customers and be able to read the spoken and unspoken clues they provide that signal how they want you to respond. Someone who delivers good customer service has what Daniel Goleman calls social intelligence. Goleman's book *Social Intelligence: The New Science of Human Relationships* outlines the attributes equated with a successful, fulfilled human being. Many of these attributes are exactly the same as the commonly cited attributes of excellent customer service. The characteristics of social intelligence and good customer service cross cultural boundaries as well. In ancient Japan, the model of service was exemplified by the intense life of the samurai. In fact, samurai means "to serve." Indeed, the person who delivers excellent customer service is in the business of serving others.

Service summary for chapter 2

- ◆ Your external customers can be individuals, groups, departments, companies, or organizations who interact with people who do belong to your organization but are not paid by your organization;

- ◆ You must understand your customers and their purpose for using your product or service if you are to deliver excellent customer service;

- ◆ The best way to understand your customers is to create a profile of them by answering three important questions: Who are they? What do they want? And how have they changed?

- ◆ Although the attributes of excellent customer service are the same across different industries, customers have different expectations about how those attributes should be delivered since their situations and circumstances are different;

- ◆ People who deliver excellent customer service have a type of intelligence called social intelligence. Through training and coaching, people can learn how to increase their social intelligence and increase their level of customer service delivery.

CHAPTER 3

FROM THE INSIDE OUT

Internal Customers

Rob, Kelly, and Warren work in the same department and all report to the same director. Rob is a financial analyst for his department. Kelly and Warren are project managers. It is very typical that when Kelly and Warren finish work on one project, the director assigns a new one. Rob works with both Kelly and Warren since they often need his help estimating project costs and revenues.

Recently, the director gave Rob an assignment requiring him to examine all past and existing projects. In addition, Kelly and Warren were just assigned new projects, and they need Rob's help to run some cost estimates so that they can get started. Kelly and Warren have e-mailed Rob, but 3 days have gone by and he has not responded. Kelly decides to walk over to Rob's cubicle to ask for his help. Kelly arrives at Rob's cubicle and finds him typing away on his computer. Kelly clears her throat to signal to Rob that she is there, but Rob ignores her cue and keeps on typing. Finally, Kelly speaks up, "Hi Rob, how are you doing?" Rob turns briefly to acknowledge Kelly, "I'm fine thanks, but I'm really busy." Rob then turns back to his computer and, while continuing to type, asks Kelly how he can help her. Kelly describes her new assignment and details why she needs Rob's help. After Kelly stops talking, Rob briefly turns around and apologizes and says, "I'm sorry, what were you saying?" Kelly is somewhat annoyed but describes the assignment again and stresses how critical Rob's help is to getting the project started. Rob breathes a deep sigh and simply tells Kelly that he is too busy at this time and cannot help. He offers no details. He does not explain that the director has assigned him a large task and she expects a quick turnaround. Kelly begins to express her surprise with Rob's curt communication, but he cuts her off in mid-sentence and reminds her again that he is very busy. He turns back to his computer and starts typing again. Kelly tells Rob a few choice words, which upsets him. Rob is now distracted from his current task of comparing old and existing projects. He is unproductive the rest of the day, and Kelly goes back to her cubicle and complains to Warren about how Rob is causing so many problems. Even more problematic than this initial disagreement is that Rob and Kelly have likely entered a vicious cycle of grudges and paybacks that will extend far beyond this confrontation.

The Kelly and Rob scene plays out on a daily basis in numerous organizations. The details may be different, but the results are the same: poor internal customer service.

Many of us have no problem giving the external customer the VIP (Very Important Person) treatment, but we do not extend the same courtesies to those we work and interact with on a regular basis. The problem is one of not viewing our coworkers as customers. Coworkers are internal customers. In fact, any person who works with you and is affected by your job—or whose job you affect—should be viewed as an internal customer. Internal customers are, in general, people who work for your same organization, division, department or group. They are the people who, in some way, have influence over and contribute to the service or product that you hope to deliver.

Organizations that focus on internal customer service find success in many ways: increased employee satisfaction, increased external customer satisfaction, and increased profits. In 1981, Scandinavian Airlines was bleeding red ink, to the tune of $8 million a year. Jan Carlzon took over the presidency of the struggling company and turned it around in 2 years time. Carlzon didn't rely on accounting gimmicks to generate $71 million in gross profit in less than 2 years. Instead, he repeated an important message to all of Scandinavian's employees: if you aren't serving a customer (external), then you should be serving someone who is (an internal customer). The essence of this message is that everyone within the company has customers. You may not interface directly with external customers, but you have internal customers who do interface with or directly impact external customers. Those internal customers should be treated with the same respect and importance as external customers.

Southwest Airlines went even further. In the 1980s, there was much ado about "The Customer is King" and "The Customer is Always Right." These slogans were clearly focusing on the external customer. Business schools around the country were assigning readings promoting this perspective and teaching their MBA students the same thing. Herb Kelleher, Southwest's founder and former CEO, turned this advice around and focused on the employees. Employees, in Kelleher's view, were the priority. Take care of the employees, treat them right, and make sure they are happy. Make sure there is an atmosphere of respect and fun. Each employee is special, and every person should treat every other person as a VIP. This is an inside out mentality. That is, take care of the people on the inside (internal customers), and they will be sure to take care of the people on the outside (external customers). Southwest's strong financial results, even in the aftermath of September 11, are a testament to the company's strong belief in taking care of employees and focusing on the internal customer.

The third ServiceElement defines and profiles the internal customer. An accurate internal customer profile can help you understand who affects your work and whose work you affect. An internal customer profile defines the interdependent relationships within the organization and emphasizes that excellent external customer service is only achieved through a team of people who deliver excellent internal customer service to each other.

Every organization has strong team members who deliver excellent internal customer service. Think for a moment about the people with whom you work. There are undoubtedly individuals on the team who you look forward to working with. They are your favorites. On the other hand, there are probably a few individuals who you avoid, if at all possible. Why do you avoid them? Probably because they provide horrible internal customer service. Now, if you wish to turn the tables a bit, ask yourself if your coworkers view you as a favorite. Do they look forward to working with you, or do they do all they can to avoid you?

Anyone who is serious about internal customer service asks these questions. And anyone who is serious about improving internal customer service, no matter how good it is now, develops an internal customer profile. An internal customer profile is built in exactly the same way as an external customer profile. Chapter 2 provides an effective three step approach for gaining insight about your external customers. This same three step approach can also be applied to gain insight into your internal customers:

- Who Are They?
- What Do They Want?
- How Have They Changed?

Most of us have not really thought about how important it is to define our internal customers. Rob and Kelly, from the beginning of the chapter, certainly do not view each other as internal customers. Rob, in particular, seems to be unaware of this concept. Rob will probably continue to ignore Kelly's request until she has to approach the director to explain why her project is stalled. Of course, Rob will deliver his own version of the story to the director. However, if Rob and Kelly view each other as internal customers, they can work together to find a solution. Their solution may not even have to involve the director. That is the power of profiling your internal customers.

Step 1: Who Are They?

Internal customers are people with whom you work. They receive their paycheck from the same company as you. Internal customers are on the inside of our company. The following list describes Internal Customers.

The list is general, but it is the first step in profiling the internal customer.

- Any person who is paid by your company and on whom you rely to do your job;
- Any person who is paid by your company and who relies on you to do their job;
- Any group, department or division within your company that you rely on to do your job; and
- Any group, department or division within your company that relies on you to do their job.

An internal customer can be an individual coworker, a group, department, or division. You must create a personal list of internal customers by asking yourself "Who are my internal customers?" Take a look at the list of the different internal customers for the four organizations shown in Table 3.1. These are the same organizations we examined in Table 2.1 (chapter 2), when we were profiling external customers.

The responses in Table 3.1 are examples that participants in our seminars cited to describe their internal customers. Notice that an internal customer must always be described from somebody's perspective. In the case of the metropolitan hospital in Table 3.1, internal customers are listed from a nurse's perspective. The nurse has many internal customers. She constantly communicates with other nurses, doctors, and physical therapists, all of whom are paid by the hospital. The effectiveness of communication among all of these professionals is directly proportional to the quality of care that the patients receive. If the nurse recognizes her internal customers and puts the effort into developing positive relationships

Table 3.1

Internal Customers for Four Different Organizations

Business Aviation Company (Chief Pilot Perspective)	Metropolitan Hospital (Nurse Perspective)	Local Credit Union (Teller Perspective)	Las Vegas Hotel and Casino (Front Desk Manager Perspective)
Pilots	Other nurses	Head teller	Front desk employees
Co-pilots	Doctors	Other tellers	Catering
Flight Attendants	Administrative staff	Business services department	Housekeeping
Mechanics	Janitorial staff		Maintenance
Dispatchers and schedulers	Physical therapists	Mortgage department	Chefs
		Front desk assistant	
Grounds crew	Billing department	Office manager	Dealers
Finance group	Ambulance services		Floor Boss
Security team			Cocktail waitresses
			General Manager

with them, the service delivery to the external customer will also improve.

It may seem odd that a nurse defines the billing department as an internal customer. Although some people may not define the administrative staff or billing department as the nurse's internal customers, those who go through the exercise of profiling their internal customers usually include these groups or individuals on their list. Patients often have concerns about billing or administrative issues. The person they feel the most comfort with is usually the nurse. Now, the nurse may not be able to answer the patient's billing questions, but if she has a good working relationships with those who can answer the questions, then she is able to help patients find the answers they seek. This certainly increases patient satisfaction and helps patients and their families make better, more informed decisions. Finally, the janitorial staff is included on the list of internal customers because the cleanliness and orderliness of the hospital is part of the patient experience and even influences the attitudes of those who work at the hospital. Janitorial staff maintains the hospital's physical environment and should also be defined as internal customers.

In addition to listing internal customers from the nurse's perspective, Table 3.1 shows that internal customers must always be defined from someone's perspective, no matter what industry we are talking about. For the aviation company, it may be from the chief pilot's perspective, though baggage handlers or front desk customer service representatives could also go through this exercise. The internal customers for the bank and hotel examples are defined from a bank teller and front desk manager perspective. Again, any person in any position, for any of these organizations, can complete this exercise, from their perspective.

Each list of internal customers illustrates the interdependent nature of coworkers and colleagues. Excellent customer service results when the concept of internal customer service is put into practice. The best way to apply the concept of internal customers to your daily practice is to begin by listing your internal customers. In Exercise 4, list five of your internal customers. Exercise 4 leads us to the next step in defining internal customers.

Building a Customer Service Culture 43

 Exercise 4

List Five Internal Customers

1. _____

2. _____

3. _____

4. _____

5. _____

Step 2: What Do They Want?

In chapter 2 we saw that external customers expect quality, experience, benefits, and solutions to their problems. They also expect good customer service. When you deliver a product or service that your external customers want or need and then go the extra mile and provide excellent customer service, you are in effect rewarding that external customer.

Internal customers like rewards as well. Internal customers also want quality, experience, benefits, and solutions to their problems. Employees and managers in today's world place a very high priority on how they feel about their jobs and their coworkers. Quality, in the case of internal customers, therefore, refers to the quality of your relationships with your internal customers. Experience has to do with whether you find meaning in your job and feel good about it. Benefits have more to do with the positive mindset that results from quality relationships with your internal customers (more on this in a moment).

Money is also a benefit, and one that can help us meet material needs or solve problems that involve payment. Money, however, is not a benefit that most of your internal customers can easily give you. For both public and private organizations, it is often difficult for managers and supervisors to provide monetary rewards, even if they think you deserve it. The state of the economy, product sales, and business needs may all dictate whether top performers are even eligible for a raise. In addition, there are many studies in the area of human motivation that underscore the limits of money on personal satisfaction. In general, we obtain job satisfaction not from money but from relationships, meaningful work, and the appreciation and encouragement that goes along with doing a good job. Money is necessary for our existence, but it does not provide true satisfaction. Dr. Gregory Berns, in his insightful book, *Satisfaction*, makes it clear that money can buy temporary happiness, but happiness is different from satisfaction. Most of us realize that our internal customers cannot give us money anyway, so what we want from our internal customers has to be something other than money.

Internal customers want quality relationships. The rewards from quality relationships at work include a list of outcomes that every internal customer finds meaningful: appreciation, encouragement, respect, friendship, and honest communication. Every internal customer likes to feel appreciated, and kind words are free of charge and have lasting impact. Words of appreciation build confidence. Often, when we are not sure of our own abilities, it is the words of encouragement from a coworker or trusted team member that helps us push forward despite our own reservations. This certainly is why encouragement ranks as an important reward for internal customers. Respect is another reward that we all desire. You have the ability to give respect to others in the way that you speak with and treat your internal customers. Those who give respect also receive it.

Everyone wants appreciation, encouragement, and respect because it leads to established friendships based on honest communication. Friendships among internal customers flow naturally as we work together over any amount of time. Some of those friendships may not extend outside of the organization, but they are nonetheless friendships. Friendships connect us with others—with a team perhaps—and thereby fulfill our need to belong to a greater whole, or a group.

Your internal customers want all of the things that are necessary to create a truly effective team, and, if you really think about what you want, it is likely that you desire these same things. The best way to deliver excellent internal customer service is the same way we deliver excellent external customer service. Take one more look at the list of Commonly Cited Attributes of Excellent Customer Service that we provided in chapters 1 and 2: positive attitude; well-mannered, attentive, and friendly; provide answers or finds the answers, but doesn't make excuses; consistency; flexibility; good communication, keeps the customer informed; personable; and quick response to questions or requests.

Excellent customer service is excellent customer service, whether it is in the realm of external or internal customers. If you practice the attributes of excellent customer service, you will be doing your part in providing excellent service to external and internal customers. If you make a habit of practicing excellent customer service techniques, these attributes become a part of you. There is power and magic in giving the VIP treatment to every person, every external and internal customer. People feel good about receiving special and respectful treatment—and not so surprisingly, you feel good about providing that treatment.

Step 3: How Have They Changed?

How have internal customers changed in terms of what they want from other internal customers? The answer: not much. As early as 1941, we formally began discovering that people really wanted recognition and quality relationships. Frederick Roethlisberger reported on some amazing studies done at a company called Western Electric. Researchers were trying to figure out what made people more productive in a manufacturing setting. After a number of years and a number of painstaking studies, researchers finally started arriving at convincing answers. In one study, for example, it was eventually discovered that productivity increases for a group of five female operators was related to whether the workers were able to talk to others (and others were willing to listen) about their concerns, thoughts, and feelings. The group of five female operators also felt recognized because they were the subjects of this national research, and this recognition by itself, as it turned out, was related to increased productivity. Some years later, in 1968, Frederick Herzberg wrote an article for the Harvard Business Review titled, "One More Time: How Do You Motivate Employees?" In this article, Herzberg discovers the limitations of money, and that it is the rewards of relationships and the work itself that creates true satisfaction and long-term productivity. People want recognition, appreciation, and interesting work. They receive these things from their team members, their internal customers.

Some 70 years have passed since some of this historical research took place, and the industrial revolution is almost gone. Yet, we continue to see the same results. Researchers in the 1940s did not understand the concept of internal customer service, but they certainly can be credited with laying the groundwork that helps us understand the concept today. The concept was always there, it was the discovery of it that took a while. In fact, we are finding the same results about what internal customer service means from our own seminars, workshops, and cultural enhancement programs. When we give seminar participants a list of rewards that includes money, appreciation, interesting work, friendships, nice office equipment, and so forth, we find that the rewards that have to do with relationships and meaningful work disproportionately surface as top priorities. Indeed, when coworkers view each other as internal customers and truly function as a team, then it is the quality of relationships and the feeling and meaning you find in your work that is most important. What was true of internal customers in 1941, since Roethlisberger's groundbreaking study, is still true today.

THE INTERNAL-EXTERNAL CUSTOMER SERVICE CONNECTION

There is a strong relationship between internal and external customer service. Consider a new company that has some investment money to create a new electronic product and proceeds to hire ten people. The 10 team members must learn how to work together both technically and interpersonally.

The team should have the required technical knowledge and skill to develop its new product. The engineers and information experts have the knowledge to develop the product, but the best ideas in the world often do not generate any profit because they are not taken to market. Clearly, the team also needs people who understand the mechanics of marketing and selling. Furthermore, in ventures such as these, finance and business analysts are needed to make decisions on costs, pricing, and production. Our new team needs a variety of people who possess different areas of technical knowledge and skill.

Technical knowledge and skill are never enough to have a well-functioning team, however. Each person on the team must know how to work with other members on the team, in essence to treat others as internal customers. The strength of internal customer service within the team will determine whether the product is developed and successful in the marketplace. The strength of internal customer service will determine whether the sales and marketing team members are able to convince external customers that the product is worth buying. This is because sales and marketing need to understand, from the engineers and information technologists, how the product works. Once external customers begin buying the product, they are going to have questions and maybe even need some technical assistance. Again, the

Figure 3.1

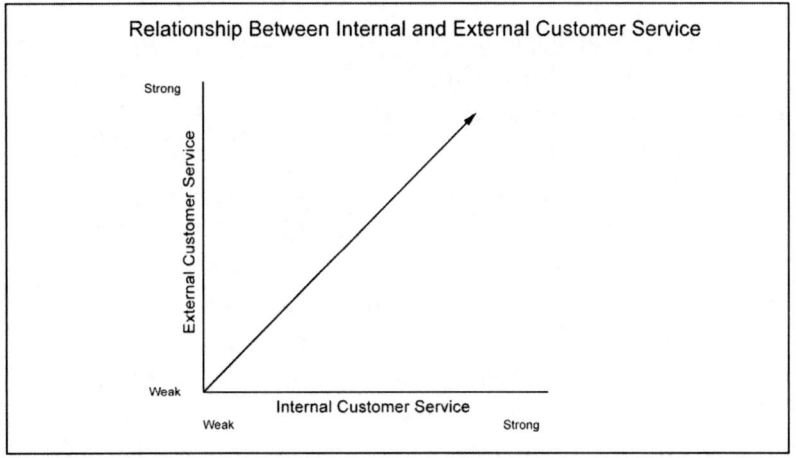

engineers and information technologists are going to have to provide some of that technical assistance. They will need good people skills to communicate with the external customer directly or with the sales person who will communicate with the external customer. Everyone on the inside of the team (internal customers) must work well together if they are to be effective with those on the outside (external customers).

Internal customer service must be strong in new companies, but it must be strong in established ones as well. As we have seen in the case of Southwest Airlines, it is the attention to the people on the inside of the company, and the level of internal customer service that each person receives, that allows external customers to consistently view Southwest as a good company with whom to do business. Figure 3.1 shows a visual representation of the relationship between internal and external customer service.

Ultimately, as Figure 3.1 shows, external customer service is only as good as internal customer service. A team of people who at first begin working together has to learn how to provide each other with strong internal customer service before they can deliver truly exceptional external customer service. In cases of weak internal customer service, it often occurs that team members end up giving the external customer two different answers to the same question, because of a mix up in communication. When internal customer service is weak, the team is too busy solving its own problems to address the external customer's problems. For all of these reasons, and many more, weak internal customer service ultimately leads to weak external customer service.

Happily, the opposite is true as well: strong internal customer service ultimately leads to strong external customer service. In an environment of strong internal customer service, external customer service becomes an effortless, natural part of the organization and people working within it. Jeff, for example, works at the restaurant, ClaimJumper's. Jeff worked in various hotels prior to joining ClaimJumper's, but he has never been happier with his job than he is at ClaimJumper's. That is because the ClaimJumper's restaurant at which Jeff is employed works hard to make sure that servers, cooks, hostesses and managers communicate and work together as a team. Jeff loves being part of a team, and ClaimJumper's gives him the opportunity to provide both internal and external customer service. It is no surprise that within 6 months of beginning his employment at ClaimJumper's, Jeff was tapped for the company's internal management program.

The relationship between internal and external customer service shown in Figure 3.1 always holds true in the long-run. It is possible, however, for a company to have weak internal customer service and strong external customer service. The problem with this situation is that the strong external customer service is not going to last very long. In the long-run, the internal division between team members will get to a breaking point, and, like a balloon that fills up with too much air, the previously strong external customer service will eventually burst into nothing. In the mid-1980s, People's Express Airlines spread its employees very thin, and they were not able to maintain workloads and communications within the team. Quality suffered and external customers were no longer willing to stand it. The demise of the airline really started on the inside.

Figure 3.2 shows the effects of different combinations of internal and external customer service on profitability. Figure 3.2 is derived from Figure 3.1. Figure 3.2 helps explain the nuances inherent in the relationship between internal and external customer service, as explained below.

Figure 3.2

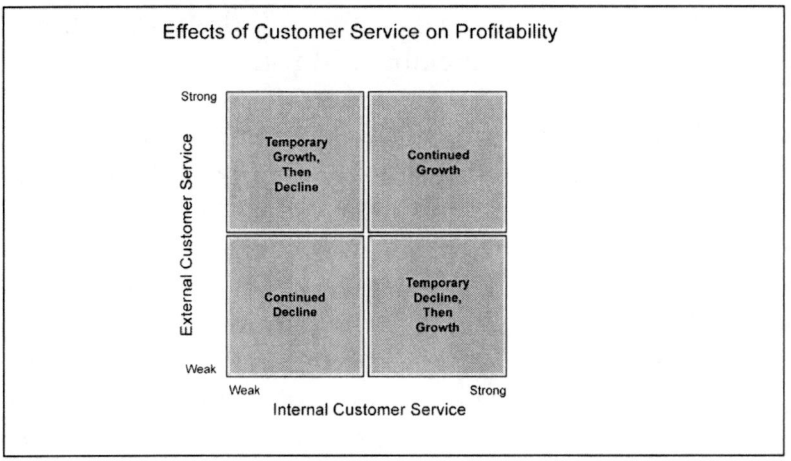

- **Strong internal customer service/Strong external customer service**: When internal and external customer service is strong, the company is profitable in terms of the bottom line or whatever goal toward which it strives. A nonprofit organization such as a university does not make money, but it is successful when internal customer service is strong and external customers such as students, alumni, and citizens feel well-served and believe the university is accomplishing its mission. Any organization with strong internal and external customer service can expect continued growth, profitability, and organizational health. The key to maintaining this position is to provide any training resources, coaching, or other tools to the team as new changes will eventually arise and temporarily challenge the team. Changes may include new competitors, changes in team membership (retirements, new hires, etc.), or new technology.
- **Weak internal customer service/Weak external customer service**: When internal and external customer service is weak, the company's decline in profitability is imminent. It is only a matter of time before the internal team self-destructs, either because team members do not get along or because they are overworked. If, as was the case of People's Express, the team members are spread too thin, internal customer service eventually leads to poor external customer service. Internal inefficiencies eventually morph into external inefficiencies. External customers soon begin voting with their feet by taking their business elsewhere. Everyone has some expectations of service standards, so cheap prices alone are not enough to sustain any business. Training may help solve some

problems when internal customer service is weak. If the problem is ongoing, it is likely that some team members are causing problems or that management is being too aggressive and not giving people the necessary time and training to learn how to work together, learn the company culture, or learn how it is that internal and external service should be delivered to every customer.

- **Strong internal customer service/Weak external customer service**: It is possible that internal customer service is strong, yet external customer service is weak. This condition is only temporary, because a team that works well together will persevere. The startup electronic company (with 10 team members) mentioned at the beginning of this section will eventually deliver strong external customer service and profitability if internal customer service is strong. Progressively, the team will become more efficient and effective. The Law of the Farm states that first one must plant the seeds and work the fields before the benefits of the harvest emerges. Similarly, a team that is committed to strong internal customer service will learn together, work together, and make any adjustments that need to happen as a result of changes they may confront. Changes in market conditions or customer expectations may cause this temporary decline. Strong internal customer service produces the teamwork and unleashes the human creativity needed to address these challenges. The team that is committed to strong internal customer service but is not yet reaping the rewards of profit and strong external customer service need only press on, for the rewards are soon to follow. Persistence is the key to achieving results. The Law of the Farm guarantees that any decline in profits or effectiveness is only temporary.

- **Weak internal customer service/Strong external customer service**: Weak internal customer service only results in strong external customer service in a limited number of cases. Further, this state is not easily sustainable, because the team or company cannot be weak on the inside and remain strong on the outside for very long. The pressures of the internal customer service problems will eventually degenerate and move the team to the bottom left (weak/weak) state of Figure 3.2. Weak internal customer service and strong external customer service usually occurs in two situations. First, companies that create a new and innovative product or service have the temporary luxury of getting away with poor external customer service. The same is true for a company that is the first to deliver a product or service to a specific market. This is commonly called the first-mover advantage. Those who move first to a new market, or create something new for the market, have an initial advantage. The problem with this situation is that new competitors will figure out your new and innovative product or service, copy it, and then provide the product or service with excellent external customer service. For example, an airline may be the first to offer direct service from one location to another, but if internal processes are so poor, external customer service eventually declines and competitors soon fill the void.

The second situation in which weak internal customer service coexists with strong external customer service is when the company initially built a good reputation by serving the external customer.

The company may have created some loyal customers, and those external customers are willing to overlook a couple instances of poor service since they are in fact loyal. Unfortunately, external customers are only forgiving for a time. As the weaknesses in internal customer service continuously spreads to external customer service, the company again moves to the bottom left-corner of Figure 3.2. In any situation, weak internal customer service and strong external customer service cannot coexist for long. Something eventually gives.

Service summary for chapter 3

- Your internal customers can be individuals, groups or departments within your organization;

- Internal customers rely on you to do their jobs, or you rely on them to do yours;

- The best way to understand your customers is to create a profile of them by answering three important questions: Who are they? What do they want? How have they changed?

- The best way to deliver excellent internal customer is the same way we deliver excellent external customer service, which is through the attributes of excellent customer service;

- The rewards that we receive from internal customer service have always existed because they meet the basic human needs for having quality relationships and creating meaningful work;

- The element of strong internal customer service will ultimately lead to strong external customer service; weak internal customer service will ultimately lead to weak external customer service.

CHAPTER 4

MOVING BEYOND SAMENESS

Visionary organizations consistently ask one very important question: Why should a customer choose my product or service? This question can be asked at the company, division, department, team, or even individual level. Furthermore, this question should be asked on a regular basis. Customers may have chosen your product or service in the past, but that does not mean that they will choose it in the future.

Organizations, teams, and individuals who ask "Why choose us?" put themselves in the customer's shoes. These organizations are self-critical and look for ways to learn—ways to improve their offerings. They are looking at their own products and services from the customer's perspective. The ability to see situations from multiple perspectives is not only a sure strategy for companies to win customers, but one that leads to success in every-

Exercise 5

Service:	Store:
Reasons for Buying this Service	Reasons for Buying at this Store
• _____	• _____
• _____	• _____
• _____	• _____
• _____	• _____

thing from professional sports and personal development to internal teamwork.

One of the best ways to see the value of this question is to start with your own experience. Why do you buy certain services or shop at a particular store? Why are you a frequent patron at a particular restaurant or hotel? Why do you feel comfortable going to the same dentist, or having your car fixed at the auto shop 10 miles from your house?

Complete Exercise 5 by following the four instructions:

1. Think of a service (any service) you currently purchase, for which you are very satisfied, and list that service on the top left-hand corner of the table in Exercise 5;

2. Immediately below the service, list four reasons why you are satisfied with this service;
3. Think of the store where you do most of your grocery shopping, and list that store on the upper right-hand corner of the table;
4. Immediately below the store, list four reasons why you shop at the store.

Look at your list of reasons for buying the service or shopping at the store you listed. There are many questions that will arise as you look at your list: How loyal are you to the service or the store that you listed? If another competitor were available, would you switch at a moment's notice? Have you passed up chances at similar products or services? Why?

Table 4.1 shows the reason many people fly with a particular airline (service) or shop at a specific grocery store. You may have listed the reasons you are loyal to a particular doctor's office or insurance company on the left hand side of Exercise 5. We picked an airline and store for illustration because these are common services peo-

Table 4.1

Service: Airline X	Store: Grocery Store Y
Reasons for Buying this Service	Reasons for Buying at this Store
• Low price	• Close to where I live
• On-time	• Low prices
• Friendly and helpful employees	• Lots of organic offerings
• Serves plenty of destinations	• Knowledgeable staff

ple mention in our workshops. We have not included any specific company names in Table 4.1, but you can see the general types of answers that people give as to why they buy from a particular airline or store. Perhaps your list looks similar to Table 4.1.

Let's first look at the airline. People almost always list cost as an important factor for choosing a particular airline. Cost is definitely important. People also like airlines that are on-time. Many pilots have a saying: If you are early, you are on time; if you are on time, you are late; and if you are late, you are left. Most of us expect the airlines to live up to the pilots' mantra. In fact, the media regularly publishes a list of the best and worst airlines on-time service. The third item under the airline, in Table 4.1, is friendly and helpful employees. This item is mentioned by just about every person who lists reasons for buying services from a particular airline. Finally, we want our airlines to provide service to many different destinations.

Now look at the column with reasons for buying at a particular supermarket. Most people shop at a preferred supermarket because of proximity and price. Bargain prices are important to most people. A supermarket is also like a gym—you use it if it is convenient and close. Organic selection has been growing on the list of reasons people shop at particular grocery stores. Even Wal-Mart is now expanding its organic product offerings to compete in this high margin market. Finally, people who regularly shop at low-priced supermarkets do not expect a lot of help from staff when making their selections, but the growth of stores that offer natural and organic products, such as Trader Joe's and WholeFoods, has somewhat changed the dynamics of grocery shopping. The product selection is vast and complex, so customers began to look to knowledgeable staff to answer questions about the food in the store. Thus, many people are drawn to organic supermarkets because of the healthy products and the staff who can answer questions about food labels or product benefits.

At this point, think back to the list you made in Exercise 5. Immediately after you completed your list, we asked you some questions regarding your loyalty and willingness to try new products or services. From a company perspective, for both the airline and supermarket, there are even more questions:

- Can we maintain our price advantage? Do we want to?
- How important are friendly, knowledgeable, helpful employees to our success?
- If we serve new destinations, will that give us a long-term, sustainable competitive advantage?
- Can we capture all of the business in this area, or will a competitor build a store across the street?
- How easy would it be for someone to duplicate our products and services?
- How loyal are our customers, and at what point would they stop being loyal?
- What is more important to our success: employees, cost, location, quality?

These are all questions you should be asking about the product or service that you provide. All of the questions really are asking the same basic thing: How do we continue to stand out? How does your organization, product, or service standout? As an employee of the organization, list five things, in Exercise 6, that makes your organization and its products and/or services standout.

 Exercise 6

Five Things that Make My Organization and Its Products or Services Stand Out

1. _____

2. _____

3. _____

4. _____

5. _____

How many of the items on your list have to do with the technical features of your product or service, or things like price and location? How many of the items on your list have to do with the quality of people on your team and how they deliver the service, how they produce the product, or how they work together to make it all happen? Sadly, in our experiences traveling around the country asking employees this very question, we find that most of them do not list the people who work in the organization as something that makes the organization stand out.

If we asked one of your competitors to make a list of five items that make his or her organization stand out, would it look much different from yours? The truth of the matter is that there are many things that we believe make our products and services stand out, but these are actually things that customers expect and that our competitors can provide. Customers expect low prices, quality, on-time arrivals, safety, functional products, fresh fruit, and easy access to your facilities. Customers expect hotel rooms to be clean, have showers and faucets with all the knobs, and a television that works.

Many times, the things that we think make our products and services stand out are the exact same things that our competitors think make their products and services stand out. When we reach the point when we are competing for customers based on the same product or service features as a competitor, then we have reached what is referred to as parity. Product or service parity means there really is no difference between products or services. This is a tough situation to be in, for when we reach parity, the customer is indifferent between our company and another one. In this situation, there aren't many ways to sustain an advantage for long, because your competitors are lurking around the corner with a new promotion or price scheme, and the customer is easily lured away. Parity means your product or service has become a commodity.

We now explain why it is a mistake to think that focusing on a particular market or competing on price or even quality will lead to a long-term, sustainable competitive advantage.

THE FALLACY OF PRICE, QUALITY OR INNOVATION AS A SUSTAINABLE ADVANTAGE

Price is often thought of as the main reason customers choose a product or service. Ask yourself this question right now: "Do I always and every time buy the cheapest product or service?" In chapter 2, the exercise of profiling the customer showed that plenty of them are willing to pay for what they want. People actually buy value as well, and they are willing to pay for it. Ninety-nine percent of our seminar participants, no matter their income level or economic capacity, tell us that they are willing to pay for value. Nonetheless, in many companies, the strategy of competing on price persists. There are four reasons why you should try to avoid competing just on price:

- Revenues will decrease;
- The business must increase its volume to increase revenue, which means that managers must squeeze more work out of each employee;
- The price advantage will soon be closed, as competitors utilize technology or other resources to "catch up" with you;
- Your product or service becomes a commodity, giving customers options outside of your offering.

Which of these characteristics is good for your organization? The answer: none of them. When you reach the point where you are competing primarily on price, you are receiving a clear signal that you have reached product or service parity. You are no longer different from the pack.

First, consider the effect of how price competition lowers revenues and creates the need to increase volume just to "stay above water." Marvin owns a business that specializes in selling home owner's insurance. The average customer requires $500 worth of annual insurance. Marvin has a steady base of 500 customers. His yearly revenue for his business is approximately $250,000. Recently, a new Internet insurance business started targeting Marvin's main customers. Everyone living in the zip code area where the bulk of Marvin's customers live started receiving e-mail advertisements and mail flyers about new insurance offers. As a result, Marvin has decided to lower his rates because he thinks it will help him keep his existing customers. Now, his average rate is $450. Marvin's strategy worked. He kept 500 customers the second year. Marvin's results for the 2 years are shown in Table 4.2.

There are many reasons why Marvin was tempted to compete on price. He saw a competitor moving in on his territory, so his first reaction was to compete on price. Marvin knows that an Internet insurance business is able to keep its costs down, because it does not require the physical space and extent of office equipment that he maintains for his business. People buy insurance from a particular company for many different reasons though,

Table 4.2

Marvin's Financial Overview

	Year 1	Year 2
Price of Insurance	$500	$450
Number of Customers	500	500
Gross Revenue	$250,000	$225,000

such as how comfortable they are with the agent who is trying to sell them a product or service. Marvin's focus on price has lowered his gross revenue to $225,000. He must now work harder to find additional customers just to make up the $25,000 he lost. That means he is going to have to find 56 new customers (56 customers will add just over $25,000 of revenue) if he wants to build his revenues back up to his year 1 level. Marvin must increase his volume of customers, from 500 to 556 just to maintain the same level of gross revenue.

If an emerging Internet competitor doesn't beat you on price, an existing, big competitor will. Wal-Mart is a formidable player in just about any grocery market precisely because it offers such low prices to its customers. Countless mom-and-pop supermarkets, along with some of the more well known chains, have struggled whenever a Wal-Mart moves into the neighborhood. Wal-Mart is legendary because it is able to offer low prices as a result of some very purposeful strategies: Wal-Mart buys vast amounts of products from its suppliers and is therefore able to negotiate discounts; Wal-Mart has an elaborate and very efficient computer system (technology) that saves it billions of dollars, further reducing its costs; and Wal-Mart saves money by carefully managing its labor costs.

No matter what your business, the story is always the same: anytime you compete on price, more work is required to maintain yesterday's revenues. You must increase the volume of business to make up for the lost revenue since you are not charging as high a price. This is equivalent to the work harder mentality. There is nothing wrong with working harder, but working smarter should always be the first option you take. If you first work smarter, you may find that you do not necessarily have to work harder. If you work smarter but still want to work harder, then your revenues will increase even more. The dangerous path is to work harder for the same or lower revenues. Indeed, for many organizations, working harder does not lead to increased revenue. Working harder may help you maintain your customers, but when you are competing on price you are fighting an uphill battle.

Most organizations, whether in business, government, or education, push their employees to work harder. "We expect more for less" is the message. Organizations start looking at hard numbers, like the amount of revenue per employee or average time per call for a customer service representative. But when we compete on price, measures like the amount of revenue per employee go down, and we push people to work harder to increase these "important" indicators of success. It becomes a vicious circle. Competing on price should never be the preferred option for avoiding product or service parity; quite the contrary, it leads right to parity. It also leads to lower revenues, which means we are pushed to work harder so we can increase volume to make up for the lost revenues. That leads to burnt out employees who feel like they are on a running wheel that was designed for rats instead of people.

PRICE, QUALITY AND INNOVATION: ALL ROADS LEAD TO PARITY

Let's say we have decided to compete on price. Our employees are willing to work harder, and they are successful in helping us gain new business to make up for the revenue that we lost because of our price decreases. In fact, we have even gained a little bit more business than expected, so our revenues have actually increased a bit. That is good news for now but bad news for later. The price advantage will not last long because someone will come along and figure out how to lower their costs. This will allow them to lower their prices and take away your customers.

In the long run, the same thing happens with a business that gets a head start on the competition by being the first to offer a product or service. In this case, the business is not competing on price since it was the first to innovate and offer a product or service. But beware. In a very short time, advantages due to innovation begin to slip away. Technology is the great equalizer, and shrinks price, innovation, or quality advantages over time. Just as technology helps us, so it also helps our competition. Robert T. Kiyosaki, in his book *Cashflow Quadrant*, describes how easy it is for the competition to catch up to you even if you were the business that invented a product or service. Kiyosaki started a manufacturing company that was one of the first to produce nylon and velcro surfer wallets that came in bright colors. The company followed with other quality, complementary products and was wildly successful. Soon, Kiyosaki's company began to weaken as competitors from Taiwan, Korea, and Hong Kong copied his products and started shipping identical products for a fraction of the cost. Even though Kiyosaki's company was the first to market with these ingenuous wallets, international competitors had the technological and manufacturing means to produce essentially the same wallet. In addition, competitors from the Far East had access to cheaper labor. Kiyosaki's company could not compete on innovation and quality for long. Pretty soon the company's competitors were producing wallets for less, which meant they could sell them for less. Eventually, Kiyosaki's company succumbed to its aggressive competitors.

There is always someone who can copy your business processes or access the same technology you use to deliver your products. Services can also be copied. NetJets is an innovative company that sells "ownership" in aircraft to corporations or anyone wealthy enough who wants to buy such ownership. The company offers customers a fraction of ownership of an aircraft by selling the remaining shares to additional customers. Each customer is thus entitled to a certain amount of flying time per year. NetJets was one of the first organizations that offered this new and quality service in the marketplace, but today there are hundreds of companies doing exactly the same thing. NetJets is still very successful, but the increase in companies supplying the same service means there are more competitors who are using the same ideas and technology, and this eventually exerts pressure on price.

It does not matter what technical advantage you start with, how innovative your product or service is, the quality of your offering, or how much you are able to drive down your price. The competition will eventually catch up with you. Your advantage, when it depends on features or price, will diminish over time. It is the Law of the Copycat, a natural law that assures copycats will catch up to you over time, as Figure 4.1 shows. The period of time in which copycats can catch you has dramatically decreased with the availability of technology and information.

Figure 4.1 shows that we may start off with an advantage because of our quality, price, or innovative offering, but that advantage diminishes over time because copycats come onto the scene. Even though the copycats start competing with you after you have been in the market for a time, they begin to close the advantage gap. Figure 4.1 only shows one copycat, but the gap closes rather

Figure 4.1

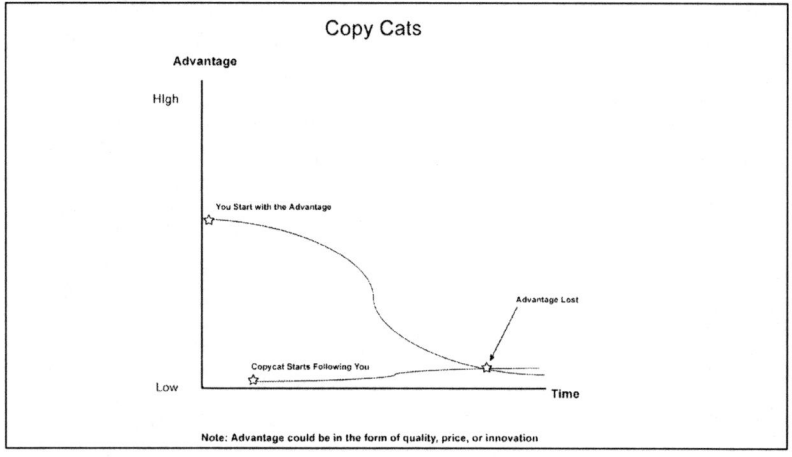

dramatically because there are, in actuality, many copycats. What is more is that all of these copycats begin understanding your market, your processes, your product or service, and your pricing. They learn from your successes and your mistakes. Once they start copying you, competition intensifies, and your competitive advantage begins to shrink. If you are not careful, your advantage will soon be lost. Quality, price, innovation, location, and countless other features can and are copied. All these roads lead to product and service parity. There is but one way to sustain your competitive advantage.

The People Differentiator

The one resource that cannot be copied is good people. The only place people are copied is on science fiction programs, and even there the duplicates are imperfect. People make the difference and can and do distinguish reputable companies from failing ones. We must assume, of course, that the features (quality, price, location, etc.) of your product or service offering are competitive. People cannot make the difference if the product or service is offered in an inconvenient location, if the price is too high, or if the quality is questionable. But assuming your product or service features are competitive, the best way to create a real advantage is through people.

In Japan, it has been widely reported that the second most important person in the company is the human resources manager. In the United States, that honor is given to the chief financial officer. In this instance, the Japanese philosophy is instructive, because it recognizes that it is through the people that true differentiation takes place. There are several reasons why real, sustainable advantage comes through the people (employees, associates, partners, etc.) who make the product or service possible:

- Customers make decisions (from external customers who buy a product to internal customers with a good attitude at work) largely based on emotions, and most of that emotion is tied to interaction with others;
- Employees can respond to existing, changing, or emerging human needs for both internal and external customers in a way that is still not technologically possible;
- Employees can listen and provide instant feedback to internal and external customers. Customers like people who listen, and they like instant feedback;

- Customer service ultimately boils down to people (see chapter 2 for the commonly cited attributes of excellent customer service).

First, and perhaps most importantly, most if not all of our choices are, at the foundation, emotional choices. We are driven by how we feel, and we make choices based on how we feel about others. Mike Hurter lives in the greater Seattle area and is one of the world's great real estate agents. Mike doesn't shortchange himself on commission and try to bargain down his commission percentage in order to get more business. Mike provides a quality service to his clients, and he charges a premium for that quality. Yet Mike is never short on business because his quality is tied to the outstanding customer service that he delivers for every client. Mike has always been a "people-person." His priority is meeting his clients' needs, and he will do absolutely anything to help his clients, including painting a house or hauling furniture to a dump. Mike gets so much business at a premium price because he makes an emotional connection with his clients. They trust and like him. The same situation plays out every day with insurance agents and countless other sales professionals. People knowingly pay higher prices if they develop an emotional connection with the seller. That is because most customers' decisions are tied to their emotions, and the best way to tap those emotions is through another person. The person providing the product or service is in the best position to build trust and establish an emotional connection with that external customer.

Internal customers also make decisions based on feelings. Have you ever known someone who really loves his job but hates everyone he works with? Most of us have known someone like this in our lifetime, but we didn't know them for very long. That is because the person didn't last very long on the job, even though he or she really liked the content of the job. If you don't get along with others, you don't last long, no matter how good you are at your job. On the other hand, people who start off disliking their jobs yet really like the people they work with, end up staying on the job longer than they anticipated. When internal customer service is high, people feel appreciated and begin to find meaning in the relationships they develop with coworkers. They begin finding meaning in their job tasks. Once again, it is the people that make the difference.

There is little doubt that technology and efficient business processes can help us improve our products and services. At the core, though, it is people who are able to respond to existing, changing, or emerging needs of internal or external customers. A computer is only programmed to follow its programmer's instructions. It cannot learn or easily respond to changing concerns or a complaint. When either an external or internal customer has a problem, it is another human being (employee or manager) who is in the best position to respond and help address that problem. People want to be heard. They want someone to listen to them. Sometimes they just want someone to listen, and other times they want someone to listen and then provide a solution. In either case, this can only be accomplished through people. Indeed, service is all about people.

WHAT DOES IT ALL MEAN?

We have seen the reasons most people give for defining why customers choose their product or service. We have also seen that most of these reasons only lead to a temporary advantage, one that weakens as copycats begin moving in on your territory. You will eventually move to product or service parity. The one true differentiator that helps you avoid parity is making a difference through people. That is why the commonly cited attributes of excellent customer service are so vital to success.

You are unique. The way that you work with others in a team is unique and cannot be repeated in any other organization. If you contribute true teamwork for the purpose of strengthening internal and external customer service, you avoid parity and create what is called a differentiated advantage. It is an advantage because it is unique, and uniqueness cannot be copied. Avoid parity by building a culture that focuses on people inside and outside the organization.

Alas, what is common sense is often not common practice. The practice of focusing on people makes good sense, yet companies that truly focus on people do not assume that this happens automatically. The common practice of focusing on people requires a steady, consistent effort. It is the individuals and organizations who focus on people that are the most successful, since they develop an irreplaceable capacity for what is known as "social intelligence." Popular author Karl Albrecht tells us that "social intelligence" can be learned. That is good news for us because it can help us avoid product and service parity. It also means everyone can develop the attributes of excellent customer service. If these attributes become a focus and a passion, then you will avoid parity and achieve true differentiation.

Service summary for chapter 4

♦ Most people mistakenly believe that product and service features are the only reason customers make purchasing decisions;

♦ Companies that focus on product and service features (price, quality, etc.) will soon find customers lured away by copycats;

♦ Copycats who offer similar product or service features push the products and services toward parity, which means there is little distinction between offerings;

♦ The true way to avoid product and service parity is excellent customer service;

♦ Excellent customer service, both internal and external, can only be achieved through people.

CHAPTER 5

MAKE TIME COUNT, DON'T COUNT TIME

As Joan is driving to work, she is going over the three items she must complete by the end of the day. Joan thinks about finishing everything before noon, which would give her time to sign up and make travel arrangements for the professional conference she wants to attend next month. As soon as Joan gets to her office she writes down her three priority items and settles in to begin the day's work. After 15 minutes, her manager, Beth, peeks in the door and says "something just came up." Joan goes to Beth's office and spends the rest of the day trying to resolve a problem for a client. At 4:30 P.M., Joan finally makes it back to her desk, with little motivation to even start working on her first priority. She checks e-mail and phone messages, looks at her mail, and then decides it is time to go home for the day. The next morning, Joan does have time to work on her priority items, which she should have completed yesterday.

Now, she is stressed and very curt with everyone who drops by her office. This makes Joan's coworkers feel hesitant to go into her office because they feel like they are intruding on her time. The month passes by and Joan does not get her conference registration or travel plans in time to get office approval. Joan simply skips the conference she was so looking forward to and resolves to make it next year. What's worse is that Beth, Joan's manager, is disappointed that Joan didn't make time to attend the conference because several important external customers always attend, providing an opportunity for networking and relationship building.

This scene plays out for countless people every day. Perhaps a similar situation has happened to you, even though the details may be slightly different. In your job, you likely experience many challenges: too much on your plate; you are expected to do more with less; you feel pulled in four different directions; or people are always interrupting you, distracting you from doing your work.

Time management experts have provided some relief by helping us organize our priorities. Although time management experts can help us manage our time more efficiently, they are not without their critics. Richard Koch, in his clever book *The 80/20 Principle*, says that the main thing time management has taught us is how to speed up our activity and fit a quart of time into a single pint. Thus, we now work harder and maybe even have more money, but we have no time to enjoy that money. Koch is a bit harsh on the time management principles, because good time management can increase productivity substantially (up to 25%, Koch concedes). When the ideas of classic time management principles are combined with insights from people like Koch and others, though, you can be more productive and improve cus-

Building a Customer Service Culture 79

tomer service, all without working yourself to death. In the rest of the chapter, you will discover how your specific activities relate to productivity and customer service.

MAKE TIME COUNT INSTEAD OF COUNTING TIME

You fulfill many roles and complete many functions on your job in a given day. It is possible that each day is a little different for you, but if you step back and look at your "typical" workday, you could probably point to several things that you do on a regular basis. In Table 5.1, describe up to ten activities that are a part of your job, in

Table 5.1

List up to ten things you do during a typical day on the job?

	Activity Description	Reactive or Proactive	Importance 1=Very Important 2=Somewhat Important 3=Not Important	Time on Activity 1=Time Intensive 2=Somewhat Time Intensive 3=Not Time Intensive	Highest Impact Activities Rank only the top 3
1					
2					
3					
4					
5					
6					
7					
8					
9					
10					

the second column with the heading "Activity Description." (You will fill out the other columns as you progress through the chapter). The things you list should include activities and duties. Use words or phrases to describe what you do during a typical day, or things that you consider to be an essential part of your job. The items that immediately come to mind should be listed without hesitation. If you have trouble listing even three items, it may be because one or more of the items you listed is too general and needs to be broken down more specifically.

Now that you have your list, examine each item closely. You will now fill out the "Reactive or Proactive" column, immediately to the right of the activity descriptions. For every activity description you listed, write down either "reactive" or "proactive" in the column immediately to the right. Put "reactive" if the activity or job you listed is something that comes up without warning. Consequently, you must react to it, since it is within your domain of responsibility. Put "proactive" if the activity or job you listed is something that you plan for. In other words, this activity or job doesn't just suddenly appear. It appears because you planned for it to appear, or you anticipated that it would appear. You were prepared. You are proactive with respect to these types of activities. Make sure each item activity description you listed in Table 5.1 is designated as either proactive or reactive, in the column immediately to the right of the description.

There are many books on time management to help you think about your activities in an orderly fashion, and most counsel that we should try to increase our proactive activities and decrease the reactive ones. These books can also give you a better sense of whether to designate a given activity as reactive or proactive. Peg Pickering's book *Prioritize, Organize: The Art of Getting it Done* and

Stephen Covey's internationally successful *The Seven Habits of Highly Effective People* are two examples of resources that utilize the concept of reactive/proactive and help us organize time by consolidating our activities into four categories. The four categories, and the essence of how they are described, are given below, though the wording and examples are fashioned to help you think about your activities and how they relate to customer service.

- **Firefighting**: Crisis mode. These are tasks and activities that must be done, but they come up suddenly and unexpectedly. Firefighting means you are devoting time to important and urgent matters, but you do not have control of the activities because you are reacting. Joan, at the beginning of the chapter, had to react when her manager asked her to help solve a customer problem. Joan did not get any of her priority items accomplished because she was firefighting the entire day. Firefighting activities are a part of every job, because it is impossible to anticipate every problem or issue that might surface. If you spend too much time in firefighting mode, however, you are a prime candidate for burnout, stress, and agitation. You will have little time to pay attention to the interpersonal relationships that are essential to maintaining internal and external customer service. Indeed, people who constantly in firefighting mode cannot maintain strong external or internal customer service for long, because the stress and agitation eventually reaches a breaking point.
- **Attention Getters**: There are a number of things, at any moment, competing for your attention. Some of these things draw your attention immedi-

ately, even if they are not important. Think about a situation where you are on the brink of solving an important work problem with a coworker—and then the phone rings. The ringing phone is vying for your attention; it is urgent, but not as important as finishing the significant headway you are making with your coworker on the resolution to the problem. Another example of an attention getter is when a salesperson has a customer who is ready to spend money on a large purchase, only to ask the customer to wait because a fellow salesperson needs help moving a box. Like firefighting, attention getters cause us to react and, as a result, lead to many of the same personal symptoms (e.g., burnout, stress). Like firefighting, people driven by attention-getting activities cannot maintain strong external or internal customer service for very long.

- **Capacity Building**: Going to conferences and training sessions takes time. It also takes time to read trade journals, or attend meetings that help you keep up with the latest developments in your field or industry. This component of capacity building is often overlooked because the ideas one gains for becoming more efficient or effective at work may not happen immediately. It may be that 2 months after a conference, you are able to apply something that you learned at a conference workshop, either to enhance communication with a customer or to improve a business process. Either way, the end result is better customer service.

Many people also consider it a waste of time to "socialize" with their coworkers, but, in fact, this is a necessary and crucial part of building trust and teamwork. What's more is that visiting with coworkers is not always just about work. Trust is built in different ways for different people, but communication is the common thread. It is also well-established that successful people spend time planning their days, weeks, months, and years. They set goals and think about how they will spend their time. People who effectively plan their week may spend as little as 10 to 15 minutes on a Sunday night doing this, before the race on Monday morning starts. But this 10 to 15 minutes is the best investment they make, because it is a proactive form of time management, which is a capacity-building activity all on its own. Contrast proactive activity with the reactive mode inherent in firefighting and attention getting activities. Proactive activities are deliberate and well thought out. Such activities avoid the traps of stress and anxiety, and thus enhance external and internal customer service.

- **Time Wasters**: These are items on your list that do not result in any productivity. If you spend an inordinate amount of time surfing the web, playing computer games, watching television, or visiting every coworker who will listen to a good story, then you may be in this category. Time management gurus will tell you that nobody really plans to waste time, so time wasters cannot be described as proactive. It would also be inaccurate to say that we are reacting to time wasters. Time wasters do not "sneak up" on us and take us by surprise, thus necessitating a reaction. We make conscious choices about how to spend our time, and most of us get a nagging feeling when we have crossed a line and are wasting too much time. If you had trouble designating any items on your list as proactive or reactive, it may be because it is a time waster. The best way to describe a time waster is "inactive."

MORE ON CAPACITY BUILDING

Our approach differs from conventional time management guru teachings on a couple of counts. First, and most importantly, it is true that you should try to be as proactive as possible. That does not mean, however, that the majority of your time will or even should be spent on capacity building activities. In fact, many jobs by their very nature are primarily reactive (think of firefighters, technical support representatives, crisis counseling, etc.). The key is to invest some time, proactively, in capacity building, through such activities as training, learning, planning, goal setting, communicating with others, and automating processes. All of these activities help you anticipate problems or better handle them when they do arise and when you do have to react. A 5-10% investment in capacity building activity can yield big rewards in terms of how effectively you handle customer issues or enhance internal interaction and productivity.

Just imagine if you spent 100% of your time in capacity building mode. You would have a lot of friends because you visited with everyone. You would also have a lot of knowledge and really great plans. You would have a lot of capacity, knowledge, and book smarts. But you would never implement anything.

Two more examples will illustrate how effective we can be by investing a strategic amount of time in capacity building. First, consider my (Mario) work as a university professor. I have learned that it is important to spend some time with employees who process travel requests and do the accounting for the university. Many professors complain that they spend unnecessary time battling with accounting, filling out reports, and resubmitting requests because a particular form was changed or a new rule was implemented. It took me some time, initially, to visit with the personnel who were handling my transactions. I also tried to get to know them on a personal basis. In fact, I even took several employees from these various departments to lunch. The employees appreciated my gesture, because they work behind the scenes and go virtually unnoticed to most people. Every person who attended my lunch had never received such an expression of appreciation from a professor, even though professors make daily requests. Ever since I took the time to establish these relationships, I have never had a single problem with accounting or the travel department. If an employee from one of these departments finds a mistake in one of my requests, the communication is always positive and the issue quickly resolved. The employees are also quick to communicate changes in accounting processes to me, or help me if I fill out a form incorrectly. In the long run, this has saved me a lot of time. I took about 3 hours to get to know the employees individually and 2 hours to take everyone to lunch (plus the lunch tab). Now, I save a lot of time because I have a good relationship with support staff and they work hard to process my requests. They remember that I took the time to thank them and to build a relationship with them.

As a last example, think about any training and educational experience, such as workshops, seminars, or coaching sessions. Many people dread training and only go because management mandates it. After conducting hundreds of training sessions across the world, we have discovered that those people who are excited about training and think of it as an investment are the highest performers. Tom works for a large corporation, and we have provided training to his organization for several years. He is always excited about training and believes that if he gets just one or two ideas from the training sessions, then his time is well spent. It was no surprise to us to return 1 year later to find that Tom had been promoted to management. After a short time in first level management, Tom was promoted up yet another level. This sort of event has happened too many times to be mere coincidence. Tom thinks of the 1 day of training as an investment, and he uses the ideas he gets to help his team function better and to improve in select areas. In turn, Tom's best employees are those who take training seriously, whether it is to build their technical skills or improve interpersonal relationships within the work environment.

From the discussion and examples, you probably noticed that capacity building takes two forms: building relationships and building technical skill. Both are important, and some would argue that relationship building is even more important than building technical skill. Building relationships requires time. People must spend time together, working on projects, talking, and visiting over lunch. Too many organizations view it as a waste of time if two employees are found visiting during "work hours." The fact is that people build trust with each other by talking about work issues, family life, and countless other topics. It is certainly a problem if you spend your whole day visiting with coworkers, but the networking and relationship building we are talking about is a normal part of any organization and should not be discouraged. Organizational theorists and psychologists actually refer to the process of building relationships as building social capital—we simply call it networking or relationship building. In a service focused organization, networking, and relationship building are two ingredients that will always enhance service delivery.

The second way to capacity build is to spend time improving your technical skills. Economists refer to this as human capital, and it is certainly an important factor in success. If you wish to build your technical capability on the job, you have to be willing to invest time in training and learning. Joan, who was referred to at the beginning of the chapter, was so busy reacting that she simply did not make that extra effort to attend a conference that could have helped her develop both greater technical skill and relationships with customers.

When you take the time to build relationships and technical skills, you will be exponentially more effective when you have to react. Malcolm Gladwell, in his book *Blink*, explains that when we have to react to something, our brains automatically rely on what we know. That could be good or bad, because in such situations you must rely on your personal experiences, knowledge, and information. The more you have learned about other people or the technical aspects of your job, the wider range of possibilities you have to draw from when you have to react to a problem. The process by which we use our instinct to react is what Gladwell refers to as the adaptive unconscious. The extent of your adaptive capacity determines how effectively you solve problems when you have to react. The extent to which you have built your adaptive capacity is the extent to which you effectively handle firefighting activities when they arise.

Though the actual amount of time you spend in capacity building activities may be no more than 10-25% of your work week, it is a crucial 10-25% of your time. It is much like the heart. In proportion to your total muscle mass, the heart is but a fraction—but it is a crucial fraction.

The Danger of Only Seeing the Trees But Not the Forest

Another score on which we differ with traditional time management experts serves as more of a warning signal than a true disagreement. We must be careful not to compartmentalize each of our tasks and lose sight of how they connect to the bigger picture. Worse, when we break down each of our tasks and make those the focus of what we do, we loose sight of the people skills that are necessary to be effective with our coworkers. We become more and more "task focused" and less and less "people focused." We begin to think of coworkers as interruptions rather than internal customers. At the extreme, we may even think of our external customers as interruptions, because they are stopping us from completing that all important task that we need to check off of our To-Do-List.

If you find yourself becoming too focused on your tasks—ever eager to check off another item on your To-Do-List—then it is almost certain that you are lost in the forest. People who are lost can only see the trees, but they have no view of the entire forest. You must be able to see both the trees and a bigger view of the forest.

In Table 5.1 you listed various tasks or activities that consume a typical workday. It is always good to break tasks down into smaller pieces. Motivational experts urge us to do the same thing when we set goals. Break a big goal into a series of smaller goals. When you break tasks, activities and goals down into small pieces, you avoid feeling overwhelmed. By breaking tasks down into manageable pieces, you define a starting point. This is all very helpful, but too often our tasks and activities become the focus of all that we do and people become an interruption. When this occurs, customer service weakens.

For planning purposes, it is effective to list our tasks and activities and then prioritize them. However, this process makes it very easy to be completely task-focused while ignoring the value of your internal and external customers. All of the tasks and activities you listed in Table 5.1 also involve people, either directly or indirectly. In reality, tasks cannot be completely separated from our internal or external customers, so we need to find a balance between focusing on tasks and focusing on people.

The Effectiveness of Inactivity

I (Bob) worked hard to grow ServiceElements into a credible and reputable company. In the early years, I worked tirelessly, constantly traveling to gain new business while also delivering virtually all of the programs that the company provided to its customers. Developing new business is an extremely difficult and time consuming activity, but it is the lifeline of any business, big or small. Developing business is urgent, important, proactive, and reactive all bundled up into one. Preparing and delivering programs and workshops also consumes a lot of time, because that is the product ServiceElements ultimately provides to the customer.

In the conduct of business development and seminar delivery, there is enough work to keep one person busy for a lifetime. But nobody can continue the frenetic pace of business development, training, and office management forever. That is simply too much time on the go.

Pretty soon either the body or spirit gives out. Eventually, I built up ServiceElements and began entrusting other people to help me deliver training and expand offerings. I can still stay busy for 70 hours a week, but I understand that an unending stream of activity can also wreak havoc on motivation and desire. I need to slow down from time to time to recharge. Motivation can become self-perpetuating and contagious, but it needs to be nurtured and reinforced by creating some time for stillness, for inactivity and rest.

If you feel your motivation and desire wane, it is possible that you have been a slave to traditional time management principles and not taken any time for yourself. We have been programmed to stay away from activities that are "Time Wasters," or those activities that are best classified as inactive. It is true that playing computer games late into the night or text messaging friends for 5 hours a day is an indication of a problem. Still, everyone needs some down time. Everyone needs inactivity, whereby they are not producing something, or working to accomplish the next big task or mark off the next item on the to do list. At ServiceElements, we teach and practice that some downtime is a very good thing, even though others may classify this as inactivity. Look at the list below to get an idea of typical items that are commonly labeled Time Wasters:

- Television viewing
- Time on the Internet
- Going to movies
- Taking naps
- Laying on the couch
- Talking on the telephone

All of the items on the list might very well be Time Wasters if you spend an inordinate amount of time on them. But done in moderation, these are not Time Wasters. You probably have a number of things that you enjoy; things that make you feel refreshed after you do them. Traditional time management practice may not encourage you to think about Time Wasters, but we do. In Exercise 7, list three of your favorite things to do that others might consider time wasters. We will take a different slant on these activities and call them Rechargers, since they rejuvenate you.

You should not feel guilty about spending time on the items you just listed. Ironically, Rechargers require inactivity but end up making us more productive in the long run. You must periodically recharge your batteries before you can be optimally productive in your life's

Exercise 7

My Favorite Rechargers:

1._____

2._____

3._____

other activities. Rechargeable batteries lose their energy after extensive use, but when they go back into the recharger for a time, they regain their energy. The same is true of people. We lose our charge if we do not include down time.

The challenge for many of us is that once we start spending time on a recharger activity, it is easy to get hooked into spending too much time on it. It is easy to channel surf and end up wasting an entire evening on the couch, in front of the television. It is easy to start surfing the Web, only to find that the morning has passed and you never really caught a good wave. Some time devoted to Recharging activities will turn out to be a proactive strategy to jump start your motivation; too much time devoted to Recharging activities turns the traditional time management gurus into accurate prophets since you will have wasted your time.

Time and Importance

Return to Table 5.1 at the beginning of the chapter. In Table 5.1, you will find a column labeled "Importance" and another labeled "Frequency." Go through each activity that you listed, and, using the appropriate scoring scales in Table 5.1 for "Importance" and "Frequency," rate each activity for those columns. Rating each of your activities on the Importance and Frequency scales will help you move a step closer to optimal utilization of your time, which produces high impact results.

Most of us hope that there is a relationship between the amount of time we spend (frequency) on certain activities and the importance of those activities. This does happen, but it is not always the case. Earlier in the chapter, we mentioned that our teachings emphasize that capacity building activities often take a small portion of time in relation to their importance. There is not a guaranteed relationship between the amount of time you spend on an activity and its importance to your job, your life, or a customer. The two corollaries below tell us that we must not assume that time consuming activities and the importance of those activities are always related:

Corollary 1: An activity that takes a lot of time is not necessarily important

Corollary 2: An activity that is important does not necessarily take a lot of time

According to the first corollary, those people who spend a lot of time doing something only to find out it is not very important end up frustrated. Ron works as a business analyst at a major company. Several years ago top management outlined a process for strategic planning. Ron was assigned to be the lead person to fill out reports and templates to complete the entire strategic planning process. Ron's other activities require him to assess business markets for certain products. Unfortunately, over the last year, Ron's strategic planning responsibilities took up the majority of his time, but the payoff was minimal. During strategy sessions, management did not meaningfully utilize the reports and templates Ron had created. Ron was left feeling that strategic planning took a lot of time but was not very important. Ron's suspicion about the strategic planning process was confirmed when management announced that it was looking at new ways of creating strategy instead of just through the traditional planning process.

Now, the second corollary says that important activities do not necessarily take up a lot of time. An example of this is capacity building. We previously mentioned that capacity building is an activity that has large payoffs (very important) relative to the modest investment in time that is required. Specific examples of the second corollary exist among very different professions. Consider the work of a police officer. Contrary to what is popularized in the movies, most police officers do not spend the majority of their shift disrupting bank robberies, engaging in hand-to-hand combat with street thugs, and exchanging gunfire in deadly shootouts. Such activities do occur in the life of a police officer on occasion, and it is critically important that the officer know how to handle such situations. So, disrupting bank robberies and fighting thugs is very important, but it is not what takes up the majority of an average police officer's day.

The work of government policy analysts provides a final example to demonstrate the truth of the second corollary. Policy analysts for federal and state government offices are highly trained individuals. Many of these professionals spend very little time testifying in front of legislators and senators, but the time when they are called upon to testify is very important. Thus, for policy analysts, there is not a relationship between time and importance when it comes to testifying in front of elected officials.

The best way to make the most of your time is to focus on the activities you rated as most "important," as opposed to those that are rated highly on "frequency." If you have an activity that is rated highly on both importance and frequency, you are truly maximizing your time.

Completing Table 5.1 will help you move beyond traditional time management principles. As you go through the process of filling out Table 5.1, it is likely that you will make one of three possible discoveries: (1) your most important activities do not take up a lot of time, but at least you are spending some time on them; (2) your most important activities are those that you spend the most time on; or (3) you are not spending the requisite time on your most important activities. Whatever the case, there exists a dynamic interplay between the various types of activities, and by thinking in terms of time *mastery* rather than time *management*, you are in a better position to be more efficient and effective with all of your customers.

The final concept that forms the basis of the fifth ServiceElement has to do with what is popularly known as the 80/20 rule, the subject of the next section.

The 80/20 Rule and Time

The 80/20 rule has been around for a long time. Over 100 years ago Italian economist Vilfredo Pareto discovered that most wealth belonged to a disproportionately small group of people. Pareto found this occurrence across different countries. Pareto observed that even if two countries had very different laws that governed tax payments, the tendency was always that a small percentage of people held the majority of the wealth (20% of the people hold 80% of the wealth).

Perhaps the most articulate and entertaining application of the 80/20 rule is by the highly pragmatic writings of Richard Koch. Koch urges us to go beyond traditional time management and apply the 80/20 principle wherever possible. Koch warns us to not get caught up in the exact percentages, but really to look at the imbalances that occur between inputs and outputs: 20% of your efforts produce 80% of the results for which you are rewarded; 20% of the people at a party drink 80% of the beer; and 20% of your carpet receives 80% of the wear.

The application of the 80/20 principle to time is the final piece of the time mastery puzzle. Turn back to Table 5.1 one last time. The very last column of the table is labeled "Highest Impact Activities." To complete this column, look back one last time at all of the activities and all the columns that you have completed on Table 5.1 so far. Make sure that you agree with all of your ratings to this point. Make any changes if necessary. Now, focus on the "Important" column. Look at all those activities that you rated as very important. You must now distinguish the very important activities. In the "Highest Impact Activities" column, assign a ranking, from 1 to 3, to those "Very Important" activities. If you had rated five items as very important, then you will have to leave two of those items out of the "Highest Impact Activities" column, because you should only rank the top three activities.

You now should have only three activities that are ranked in the last column. These three activities should be the focus of your efforts, particularly your top ranked activity. The top three activities that you ranked will produce at least 80% of the results you receive, so it is necessary to make time for these activities. Now that you have completed Table 5.1, answer the questions in Exercise 8.

You must ensure that you make time for your Highest Impact Activities. Practically speaking, you may have to spend a lot of time fighting fires and answering urgent requests, but the process you have completed by filling out Table 5.1 will help remind you that you must make time for your highest impact activities. In the long-run, your highest impact activities will produce at least 80% of the results you achieve for your efforts. Make sure that all of your efforts are working toward the results you hope to achieve. Make sure that even your activities that are lower in importance contribute to your high impact

 ### Exercise 8

Are most of your activities proactive or reactive?

_____

_____

Is there a match between the amount of time you spend on certain activities and the importance of those activities?

_____

_____

What are the things you can do to guarantee that you have time for your Highest Impact Activities?

_____

_____

activities. For example, if you must attend a luncheon, be strategic about who you sit by. Perhaps there is someone at the luncheon who can help you solve a problem or address a customer issue. In this way, you are building social and technical capital. There are opportunities that pass us by on a daily basis. People who understand which activities produce the most results consciously look for opportunities in what may at first appear to be reactive or wasted time. They invest quality time, moving beyond the singular focus on efficiency that is the cornerstone of traditional time management. High impact activities may not have an immediate result, either. But those who proactively build capacity or address a concern do much to cut off customer service problems before they even surface.

Service summary for chapter 5

- Traditional time management principles will help you be more efficient, but be careful about putting tasks above people;

- Make sure proactive activities are priorities and that you spend some time on them, even though the majority of your time may be spent on reactive activities;

- Break tasks down, as traditional time management experts advise, but make sure that each small task is helping you toward your larger goals;

- Take time to be inactive;

- Find your highest impact activities—those 20% of activities that yield the highest results—and make sure you spend focused time engaged in them.

CHAPTER 6

CYCLE OF SERVICE THINKING

All great ideas are the culmination and synthesis of prior ideas and inventions. Henry Ford certainly found success mass producing the Model T on an assembly line, but Ford alone did not invent the automobile or the mass production line. First, consider the automobile, for which no one person can take credit for "inventing." The use of the wheel preceded the invention of the automobile. Ancient societies long used the wheel to make work easier, moving materials from one place to the next. As technology progressed, people began riding bicycles. Wheels naturally found their place to the automobile. The combustion steam engine used by Robert Fulton's boat was another piece of the technology puzzle that eventually contributed to the success of automobiles. Virtually every component in the automobile required previous innovation and applications of that innovation. The story of mass production is the same as that of the automobile in that there was much groundwork that had to be laid before Ford could mass produce his Model T to revolutionize the world.

Innovation in customer service also relies on prior ideas. It is the creative person or organization that takes those ideas and marries them or combines them with ideas from other areas of business and education to produce truly valuable insight. Consider the intriguing idea of "a Cycle of Service." A Cycle of Service is simply a series of events that, when put together, delivers something meaningful to the customer. The Cycle of Service concept has a relatively new history, but there are several past ideas upon which it is built. Jan Carlzon, for example, drew attention to how our actions influence customer perceptions and gave us a new vocabulary to think about these concepts, as we will discuss momentarily.

The Cycle of Service has roots in the explosion of the service economy, which gained momentum long before its prominent influence in the 1980s and 1990s. When people think about the 1960s and 1970s, they think about manufacturing. As a country, it was in the 1980s and 1990s when we really began thinking about the role of services as a competitive advantage. At about the same time, it became difficult to classify different types of business under old categories from what is called the Standard Industry Code (SIC). The SIC system is confining because it fits best with an industrial, manufacturing view of the economy. Today, service industries are widespread and a dominant part of our economy; and massive organizations that we assume make their money selling products sometimes make even more selling services. Ford and General Motors may sell automobiles, but they also make a lot of money financing them. The well-deserved attention to service has encouraged management gurus, academic experts, and everyday employees to begin thinking about the events, activities, and processes contributing to a customer service encounter.

The scientific methods developed around the quality movement, by Joseph Juran and Edward Deming in the early and mid-twentieth century, proved to be another valuable link in the chain for improving our understanding of the Cycle of Service. Deming and Juran developed the ideas and concepts of the quality movement, one of which is called process mapping. The concepts of process mapping help improve efficiency and create improvements and are captured within the standards of movements such as Six Sigma and ISO 9002 (the ISO 9000 series is a family of standards for quality management systems, which is maintained by the International Organization for Standardization).

Process mapping has been used extensively in manufacturing environments to visually map out the series of steps that occur on a manufacturing line. By mapping out these steps in detail, it is possible to find out where real or possible problems occur. Sometimes mapping the manufacturing process may not even reveal any problems, but it might indicate how the process might be made more efficient. This is possible because the mapping helps point out critical bottlenecks or errors in the process, or it can help detect where potential problems are likely to surface.

Process mapping is also a valuable idea that can be applied to customer service. A Cycle of Service, as stated earlier, is simply a series of events, that when put together, delivers something meaningful or useful to the customer. Since the cycle includes many events, it is important to define each of the events that contribute to the cycle. Just as different steps can be defined on a manufacturing line, so too can different events be defined in a Cycle of Service. Each of these events produces what may be called a Moment of Truth. Jan Carlzon, the former CEO of Scandinavian airlines who brought the notion of the internal customer to the forefront, is also credited for helping us think about Moments of Truth. A Moment of Truth is an event within a Cycle of Service and is so called because it is at this moment that the customer begins to make decisions or develop impressions about the quality of our service. During a Moment of Truth, an employee or the company in some way comes in contact with the customer. Carlzon once said his company had 50,000 Moments of Truth every day.

A Cycle of Service may include 3, 4, perhaps 10 Moments of Truth, but within every cycle there are often 1 or 2 Moments of Truth that are especially important in shaping customer perceptions. Positive customer perceptions eventually produce customer satisfaction and hopefully customer loyalty; negative customer perceptions eventually produce complaints, negative word of mouth, and a loss of customers.

An especially notable Moment of Truth is called a Critical Moment of Truth. A Critical Moment of Truth may determine whether a customer uses your service again or goes and tells ten other people not to use it. The best way to ensure that the Critical Moment of Truth is a positive experience for the customer is to make sure we are meeting or exceeding the customer's standards and expectations. Thus, the final step in a formal Cycle of Service analysis is to define a Standard of Excellence for each Critical Moment of Truth.

A few examples will demonstrate how you can identify a Cycle of Service and go through a helpful analysis to ensure you are creating customer satisfaction and loyalty. Perhaps you enjoy going to the movie theatre. The movie going experience is one that many people enjoy. The Cycle of Service for going to the movies is something most people can relate to. First, before you even walk in the theatre, the Cycle of Service begins. You must find parking. Parking is the first Moment of Truth. Is the parking lot of your local movie theatre small or spacious? Are there spaces for compact cars as well as oversized vehicles? Do you often have to park across the street and cross a busy intersection to get to the movies? Within that first Moment of Truth for going to the movies, you as a customer form many impressions and opinions regarding your movie going experience.

The next Moment of Truth, after you park your car, occurs at the ticket office. You must buy your tickets to the movie, and theatres structure their lines differently, leading to different customer reactions. Some theatres have multiple windows open and require you to choose a line. Normally, you follow a process similar to when you are at a grocery store: first you assess how many people are in each line, and then you try to discern whether the cashier is leisurely or efficient. After you have made these assessments, you then choose your line (and for some reason or another, it usually ends up being the slowest line). Some movie theatres do not require you to choose a line, because they have arranged their lines much like a bank. There is one long line and multiple cashiers. You do not know which cashier you will get because the cashier who finishes first will call you when you are at the front of the line.

As you can see, there is a lot to a Cycle of Service. You have not even watched the movie, and already your perceptions and opinions about the service you are buying are hard at work. After you purchase your tickets, there are at least five more Moments of Truth: concessions, seating in the theatre, the actual movie-viewing experience, restroom usage after the movies, and your final return to the parking lot.

Once all of the Moments of Truth are identified, the task then turns to identifying the 1 or 2 critical moments. It is very easy to identify a Critical Moment of Truth by asking a simple question: Which Moment of Truth has the most potential to satisfy the customer or drive him away? In the case of the movie-going experience, the movie-viewing experience certainly qualifies as a top candidate for the Critical Moment of Truth.

Now that you have identified the Critical Moment of Truth, you must set a Standard of Excellence. The Standard of Excellence may create a new process, a standard operating procedure, or perhaps a measure to ensure that the customer's expectations are met. Theatre management cannot control whether every viewer is going to like a particular movie, but there are several Standards of Excellence that will serve to ensure that the movie-watcher is satisfied with the movie experience:

Standards of Excellence for Movie Going Experience

- Every theatre is to be thoroughly cleaned by at least two staff members at the conclusion of every movie;
- All theatres within the complex will have stadium seating within the next year;
- All movies will have digital sound;
- A staff member will walk up and down the isle every 15 minutes to ensure there is no unnecessary talking or unruly behavior that might disrupt the pleasure of the movie-going experience for any customer;
- Other standards defined by staff.

The example of the movie going experience provides an excellent illustration of the Cycle of Service. Of course, it is entirely possible to take each Moment of Truth and set a corresponding service standard. For example, perhaps management has received numerous complaints about the cleanliness of the restrooms. Most customers visit the restroom right after the conclusion of their movies, but it may not be necessary to define four or five service standards for this particular Moment of Truth. An effective service standard for the Moment of Truth of "restroom usage" may simply be setting up a schedule that demands every restroom is cleaned every 2 hours. Simple but effective. If you identify a Critical Moment of Truth, it will help you focus on the most important event that wins customer satisfaction and loyalty. The Critical Moment of Truth is the priority and the starting point, but given time and diligence, you can also give the necessary attention to the other Moments of Truth. The significance of providing simple standards means that there is a large payoff because these standards define things that are easy to correct or implement. In addition, simple standards are easy to communicate to customers and employees. Finally, simple standards proactively encourage actions that will help you avoid potential customer service problems in the future.

Table 6.1 is a template to help you apply the power of the Cycle of Service concept. Our own customers have told us that simple is better, and that the Cycle of Service Template is an easy way to map activities and events and define standards of excellence.

The template in Table 6.1 can be applied to any organization and any activity; it does not matter if you are selling cars or designing an automated phone menu to answer customer inquiries. Wherever you apply the

Table 6.1. Cycle of Service Template

Select An Individual Cycle of Service at your organization:

_____

Moments of Truth in this Cycle of Service:

1. _____

2. _____

3. _____

4. _____

Critical Moment of Truth is When:

_____

_____

_____

Set the Specific Service Standard:

_____

_____

_____

Cycle of Service Template, we always recommend that team members work on the template together and complete it from the customer's perspective. This strategy helps you get into the mind of the customer and view the experience through his or her eyes, which means you are objectively evaluating your own service.

As an example of how to apply the template, let's consider air travel, specifically for customers who charter aircraft to get to their destinations. Before we get too far with this example, a little background on companies that charter jets and the customers who buy their service may help set the stage. In the business aviation industry, charter management companies are experiencing tremendous growth. Charter management companies charter out aircraft for clients who prefer not to fly on commercial airlines. These customers typically have the money to buy a flight to wherever they wish to go. Such customers are among the most demanding and discerning customers one can find. For example, CEOs who charter aircraft have done so because they do not want to wait in line at an airport for a commercial flight, nor do they wish to arrive 2 hours early to avoid the dreaded middle seat. These customers are paying a high price for a private aircraft because they believe their time is worth that price. People who purchase travel from charter companies can show up 15 minutes before their flight, thus saving a lot of time. Customers who charter a flight can afford many things in life, so they typically have very high expectations as well. The smallest slip in customer service may be very expensive, as charter management customers have been known to demand a complimentary trip just because of the smallest oversight.

There are actually three distinct Cycles of Service that occur during a trip in which air travel is chartered by the customer: Customer Arrival, Inflight, and Destination

Arrival. These three cycles must be broken down into Moments of Truth. Table 6.2 shows a Cycle of Service Template for Customer Arrival at a charter management company, to demonstrate how to use the template. Notice that a Critical Moment of Truth has been identified, along with one simple service standard.

The Cycle of Service template is most useful if it provides enough detail to be meaningful but not so much that it is stifling. Within Customer Arrival, for example, we have four Moments of Truth, as shown in Table 6.2. Our charter customers are the type of people who are used to having their needs met immediately, and they

Table 6.2. Cycle of Service Template

Select A Cycle of Service:

Customer Arrival

Moments of Truth in this Cycle of Service:

1. Parking or Customer Drop-off

2. Lobby Entrance and Greeting

3. Baggage Handling and Trip Debrief

4. Boarding Aircraft

Critical Moment of Truth:

Lobby Entrance and Greeting

Set the Specific Service Standard:

There will always be someone, either a receptionist or crew member, to greet customers upon entrance into the lobby within the first minute of their arrival.

never expect to wait for anything. Thus, the Lobby Entrance and Greeting has been identified as the Critical Moment of Truth in this example. Most companies have a lobby that customers enter prior to boarding their flight, and the lobby is thus an important factor in shaping initial perceptions. In the charter business, you do not get a second chance to make a first impression. The service standard is that every customer will be greeted within one minute of arrival and escorted to the appropriate waiting area. Different companies may have different ways of making sure this service standard is met. In one company, a receptionist or customer service representative is always present at the lobby desk, ready to greet and direct anyone who walks through the door. At another company, even more insurance is added: if the receptionist is on the phone or there is more than one customer, the receptionist can press a button on the phone that alerts someone in the back offices that help is necessary—and anyone, including managers, will respond to the call for help so that the customer is not left unattended. Service standards can be met in many ways, and employees will always feel more ownership and try harder to meet the service standards if their ideas are part of the solution to meet those standards.

Several hints will help you apply the Cycle of Service Template in a way that maximizes customer satisfaction and loyalty. First, do not define too many Moments of Truth, Critical Moments of Truth, or service standards. If you were to identify 20 Moments of Truth, 10 Critical Moments of Truth, and 7 service standards for each Critical Moment of Truth, the template would be unwieldy and lose its utility as an improvement service tool. Remember, simple is most usable; and simple, common sense ideas lead to hassle-free, excellent customer service.

Second, the Cycle of Service Template is a group effort. The template will strike the appropriate balance between comprehensiveness and simplicity if different people are involved in creating it. We would warn that this is a process, however. Teams often define too many Moments of Truth, but if the team process is properly managed, consensus usually develops around a reasonable number of Moments of Truth, critical moments, and service standards.

Finally, and perhaps most importantly, any given Moment of Truth may in itself be a Cycle of Service, depending on your perspective. One of our favorite activities in our seminar and workshop programs is to break participants into groups of three or four and look at the Cycles of Service Template from different perspectives. For example, if we are working with a group of pilots, flight attendants, and customer service representatives at a charter management company, we ask them to assume that they work as Baggage Handlers. Notice from Table 6.2 that Baggage Handling is one of the four Moments of Truth. The task, then, is to assume that "Baggage Handling" is not a Moment of Truth, but a Cycle of Service all on its own. From this perspective, Baggage Handling has several Moments of Truth (taking baggage from customer, checking tags, transporting bags to aircraft, etc.). Pilots, flight attendants, and customer service representatives often come up with excellent templates for Baggage Handling once they walk in the shoes of the baggage handlers and view the process from the eyes of the baggage handlers. The point of this exercise is not really to get this group of employees to tell those who handle baggage how to do their jobs, but rather to gain an appreciation for the detail involved in every job where interaction with customers (or their belongings, in this case) has the potential to contribute to or take from an excellent customer service experience.

Carlzon identified the Moment of Truth concept in 1987, and many have added to his groundbreaking insight. Now, over 20 years later, these ideas have more relevance than ever before. How many moments in the day are you shaping or influencing your customers? The purpose of the Cycle of Service Template provided in Table 6.1 is to help you identify a process that is important in the delivery of excellent customer service. The initial template may be very simple, but most people begin to unearth service gaps and problems in their organizations by using this practical tool. If a particular Moment of Truth is creating a problem, then two possible solutions exist: (1) define it as a Critical Moment of Truth and set a service standard for it; or (2) define this not as a Moment of Truth, but as a Cycle of Service, and break it down into more detailed Moments of Truth to uncover the problems that lie deeper below the surface. In either case, recruit a variety of people to work on your organization's Cycles of Service. In doing so, you will view your own services from a fresh perspective and dramatically increase the chances of improved service delivery and increased customer loyalty. At the same time, you will contribute to the enhancement of your organization's culture, helping it transform into a customer service centered culture that ensures ongoing success.

Service summary for chapter 6

- The Cycle of Service Template is an analytically based tool that complements the interpersonal skills that are needed to deliver excellent customer service;

- Simple is best: define a manageable number of Moments of Truth, Critical Moments, and Service Standards;

- When defining Moments of Truth, it is best to look at the situation through the eyes of the customer;

- Service Standards should be specific, but the means by which those standards are met can vary;

- If a Moment of Truth or a Critical Moment of Truth is particularly troublesome, make it a Cycle of Service so that you uncover more detail and get to the real problem;

- Involve several people in the process of filling out the Cycle of Service Template, making it a vehicle by which to enhance the service culture in your organization.

CHAPTER 7

BEYOND CUSTOMER EXPECTATIONS

Customers can be a finicky lot. They expect to have a memorable experience. Customers will be quick to examine your product or service against other offerings, and technology allows them to make almost instantaneous comparisons. Part of the reason why EBay is so effective is because buyers can look to see if others have had problems with a particular seller. If that seller has cheated previous customers or sold a problem product, potential customers will certainly see a low rating for that seller. That is the power of information and technology, and it is one example of how both are driving customer expectations to ever higher levels. In short, today's customers have unprecedented choice in an ever growing and competitive marketplace.

A powerful reality of customer service, however, is that despite all the choices and the increasing power of the customer, the informed business still has a few tools left to attract and retain customers. It is still possible to turn your customers into what Ken Blanchard has termed "raving fans." Customers love to compare products and services, but they also tend to stay with a particular product or service once they have made a choice. That is the value of the repeat customer. People do not like to continuously switch to new products or services because any new product or service is unfamiliar, in one respect or another. We all become comfortable with what we know, and there is an element of discomfort involved with trying something new. It also consumes time and effort to get used to a new product or service. It is extremely difficult to switch from using a PC to a Mac, for example, even though Mac disciples swear by its superiority. For many of us, it is even difficult to order something new off the menu of our favorite restaurant, even though we have been visiting that restaurant every other week for the past 5 years. Colorful coupons and newspaper ads are intended to lure us to a new supermarket, but it is hard to leave our old store because we know the order of the aisles and the chirpy store manager. The risk in switching from one thing to another often is not a matter of money but one of psychological comfort. We all like predictability and routine because it provides the psychological comfort which we all seek.

The key to creating psychological comfort for your customers lies in unlocking the relationship between customer satisfaction and needs and expectations. A need is a natural or self-prescribed requirement. Expectations emanate from our needs. In today's world of technological capability and 24/7 access, we all expect companies, sellers, and even family and friends to meet our needs. When we expect someone to meet our needs, it is because we want good or profitable outcomes. If our expectations are met, we are usually happy and satisfied;

and if they are not met, we are usually disappointed and upset because we have not gained good and profitable outcomes.

Most of us believe that satisfaction is a natural result of meeting expectations, hence the idea of customer satisfaction. But there are times when someone meets our expectations but fails to satisfy us. This usually happens when we have been carrying the expectation with us for some time, anticipating that someone would meet it. Time goes by, and still the person (or business) does not meet the expectation. Finally, they meet our expectation, but we have been waiting so long that we are angry and upset rather than grateful and satisfied (more on this later, but for now imagine your food arriving 45 minutes after you ordered it).

Somewhat counterintuitive is the possibility of creating satisfaction without meeting expectations. Recall that expectations come from our needs. There are two types of needs: conscious and unconscious. People formulate expectations exactly because they are conscious of their needs. I need tasty food, so I expect the restaurant down the street to provide it. There are some needs, however, that we do not consciously think about because the need may not be urgent, immediate, or properly formulated in our minds. Expectations develop from conscious needs, but with unconscious needs, the expectations lay dormant. If you make a customer aware of an unconscious need and then meet that need, you will likely create satisfaction for that customer. A good deal of marketing and advertising is designed to create a need or help bring the customer's need to the conscious level. Then, fortunately and not so coincidentally, the company that is doing the advertising has the solution for meeting the need. When you find yourself wondering how you ever did without a product or a service, then it is likely that the companies selling the product or service have done a good job bringing our unconscious needs to the surface. Cell phones are a good example. They tap the need for anytime, anywhere communication with loved ones or business associates.

The businesses that will thrive in the future are those that understand the connection between satisfaction and needs and expectations. Successful businesses will also have a healthy concern about informed and savvy customers moving to the competition—something referred to as "healthy paranoia." Healthy paranoia provides the motivation for organizations to create exceptional service experiences since they work hard to understand their customers' needs and by doing so are in an excellent position to meet expectations and create satisfaction. Figure 7.1 profiles four different customer types, by whether their expectations were met or unmet, and whether their satisfaction is high or low.

Figure 7.1

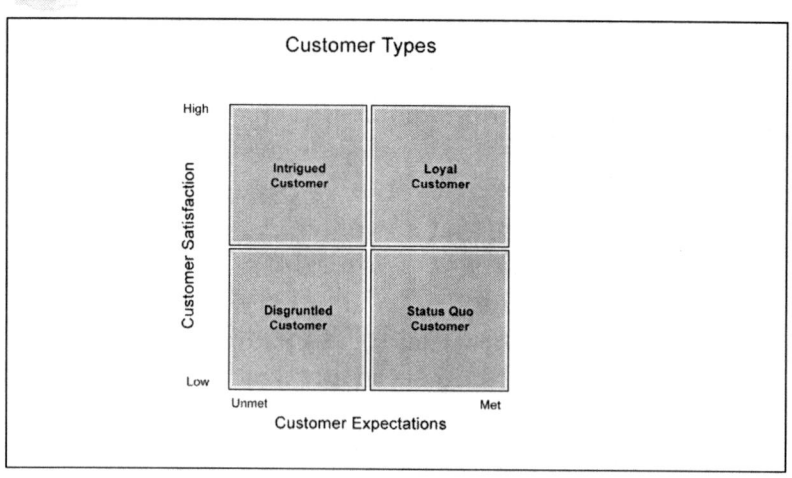

Loyal Customer

The best possible scenario for any business is to meet the customer's expectations and create high satisfaction. The source of a loyal customer's high satisfaction level is related to expectations. Expectations are clearly met in this case, but the loyalty is created when the service in fact exceeds expectations. The good news is that there are many opportunities to exceed customer expectations simply because so many businesses and the people who work within them do not practice the common sense attributes of excellent customer service or make the effort to really know the customer.

Jiffy Lube provides an excellent example of creating high satisfaction by meeting and then exceeding expectations. A customer who has never been to Jiffy Lube might expect that the oil change will be done in a "jiffy." So, if you are a new customer at Jiffy Lube, your expectation centers around a short wait time for your oil change. What you actually find at Jiffy Lube is much more. The workers are very informed and friendly. They not only change your oil but they check myriad of other issues related to the maintenance of your vehicle. You never feel pressured to pay for extra maintenance, but you are informed. You can also rest assured that Jiffy Lube's computer system will track all of your maintenance for you so that you don't have to do it yourself on the manual that came with your vehicle. At the end of your jiffy visit, you will also find that your vehicle has been vacuumed and the windows cleaned. Jiffy Lube also continues to push itself to exceed expectations for repeat customers. Jiffy Lube workers have taken a page out of the Ritz-Carlton Hotel's playbook and applied it to their business. Ritz-Carlton always amazes customers by "somehow" knowing the name of the customer before he or she even checks in at the front desk (all we will say is a quick sense of awareness and a little technology go a long way). At Jiffy Lube, don't be surprised if you drive up the next time, as a repeat customer, and the technician who greats you already knows your name. Again, a quick sense of awareness and a little bit of technology is the key to the secret. Dale Carnegie told us a long time ago that the sweetest sounding word to any person is his or her own name. Ritz-Carlton and Jiffy Lube are creating psychological comfort and security by building this into their customer service experience, and with it customer loyalty.

Loyal customers are repeat customers and strong word of mouth advocates for your business. The ultimate service achievement is to create loyal customers. This involves creating and innovating on the customer service end to differentiate yourself from your competitors. The product or service must always be at or above standard, but building customer loyalty often rests in the small things that a company or organization does to tap the human sense of happiness, fulfillment, and security.

Status Quo Customer

Many businesses assume that if you meet the customer's expectations then nothing else remains. The problem with this mindset is that it assumes that a customer who has his expectations met is also a satisfied customer. This is not necessarily the case, because expectations and satisfaction are not always the same, especially when it comes to customer service. Those businesses that have mostly Status Quo customers are those businesses that do enough to get by—but no more. We should guard against measuring our service performance based on the minimally acceptable level of service the customer will accept. Such performance is based on the lowest common denominator of performance and will not produce loyal customers.

Studies in human behavior have long shown that once a desire is met, it soon becomes an expectation that no longer motivates. Similarly, if you get something you were expecting in the first place, it certainly will not motivate you. Imagine, for a moment, that you have been working long, hard hours over the last year on a special project at work. Your performance has been stellar, but you believe you have long been due a raise. Months go by and you do not get your raise. Finally, 6 months later, and many additional weeks of working over 50 hours, your manager approaches you and announces that you are receiving a raise. For most people in this situation, the raise will not motivate them to work harder if they had been expecting that raise for some time. In this situation, most people will actually think "Well, it's about time I got my raise!" The raise was expected, and it does nothing to motivate in the future.

Customers are often the same way: if you provide something they expect, they may not be as satisfied and happy as you may have thought. They definitely will not be motivated to tell others about your great products and services, and their return as a repeat customer is not even guaranteed. They may not complain, but they will not be a raving fan for your business. If you simply meet a customer's expectations, then you have done nothing to distinguish yourself from the competition. One does not gain loyal customers by only doing what is expected. After all, everyone expects quick, friendly service wherever they go—that is the baseline of customer service. Everyone expects the product they purchased at the local electronics store to work once they plug it in at home. Everyone expects their restaurant order to be cooked exactly as they asked for it, and in a timely manner. Everyone certainly expects that the plane ticket they purchased will get them safely from one city to another, with little to no inconvenience.

We should not assume that a customer will be satisfied just because we met his expectations. We should also strive to provide more than just psychological comfort if we wish to create true customer satisfaction. Many customers go back to a business only because they are comfortable and know what to expect. After all, that is how McDonald's has grown internationally. You may not particularly care for a Big Mac, but at least you know what to expect if you spot a McDonald's while in Russia. The danger with the Status Quo customer, though, is that he is like the tourist in Russia who eats at the recognizable establishment because it is predictable. If something else comes along that catches his interest, he will easily go along with that something else. The only thing keeping a Status Quo customer is familiarity, predictability, and an aversion to risk. The Status Quo customer is psychologically comfortable with your product or service, but a convincing "teaser" or slick advertisement is all it takes to convince him to try something else. Building business on Status Quo customers is risky business indeed.

Intrigued Customer

Imagine that you had never heard of the talented director M. Night Shamalyan, but agreed to accompany me to his latest movie. You had no expectations because you did not know anything about Shamalyan's previous movies or that he had directed the wildly popular movie *The Sixth Sense*. As we take our seats and the movie progresses, your need for entertainment is fulfilled with each major scene. You are intrigued after the movie, even though you had no expectations to start with. In fact, you are interested in seeing more of Mr. Shamalyan's work after seeing this movie. You leave the theater fully satisfied, even though you had no expectations. The movie fulfilled your need for entertainment even though you had no conscious expectation that it would do so.

It is impossible to meet the expectations of any customer who comes to us with no expectations, but that does not mean we cannot meet a need for this customer. How? Intrigue this customer by creating a need and then fulfilling it. A need is deeper than an expectation, so we can win big by first creating a need and then fulfilling it, all before our customers even consciously define their expectations. Clearly, in these cases, expectations and needs are two different things. It is only after the customers have these newly created needs fulfilled that they will then expect us to fulfill them the next time as well. Hopefully you are prepared to fulfill your customers' needs if you are going through the trouble of creating them in the first place. The ultimate strategy as a provider of products and services is to be able to define the need and then fulfill it, because doing so creates a satisfying and memorable customer experience.

We pay money for products and services without any expectations for a variety of reasons. A corner grocery store may have a convenient location, so you shop there simply because of the convenience but really have no expectation of exceptional service or product offerings. If you find out that the grocery store offers organic bacon products, which is something you did not expect, your satisfaction may well increase. In fact, you now may be curious enough to become a more faithful customer because you may find additional organic products on your next visit. As another example, consider the use of humor on Southwest flights. People certainly don't expect to be entertained by flight attendants telling funny jokes or singing songs, but when Southwest flight attendants started doing this, they created interest and laughter that generated a positive buzz for the airline. After the clever jokes, people unconsciously lighten up and have a relaxing flight because Southwest has created and met a need for laughter and happiness. They have also met the psychological needs of many passengers by reducing anxiety for those who are nervous about air travel. There really is no better way to generate positive word of mouth than meeting the very need that you created in the first place. If you are able to create and meet a need, you are able to create a satisfying customer experience.

The intrigued customer is almost as valuable as the loyal customer. The intrigued customer will talk about your product or service because there is an element of surprise or curiosity. The human propensity to excitedly discuss surprising and curious events is the equivalent of a multimillion dollar advertisement campaign. Even though companies may not be able to intrigue customers forever, that initial intrigue may convince the customers to try your product or service again so that you have the chance to win them over as a loyal customer.

Disgruntled Customer

It seems unlikely that any business could survive when a good number of its customers are disgruntled. After all, disgruntled customers have low levels of satisfaction and their expectations are not being met. Imagine that you have bought a health insurance plan that requires you to see a particular physician (primary care physician) who manages all of your care. You have been experiencing discomfort in your chest over the last few weeks, so you call for an appointment. The physician is not able to see you for a couple of weeks, but you make your appointment anyway. The day of your appointment finally arrives, and you get to the doctor's office, only to wait 2 hours. You have many questions for the doctor, but when you finally make it into the examination room, 15 minutes are spent with the nurse and only 5 minutes with the doctor. The doctor is hesitant to refer you to a cardiologist and quickly prescribes some medication that he says may help. His advice is to give the medication a week to take effect, but if it doesn't work, he instructs you to make another appointment to figure out the next step. You leave feeling like the doctor did not listen to you. You expected to get permission to see a specialist. But you need your primary physician's permission, which you did not get in the 5 minutes you saw him. Your entire experience is unsatisfying, and your expectation of receiving proper care and comfort goes unmet. Not surprisingly, you are disgruntled.

Sadly, some businesses operate with little regard for the customer. The profile of a business with little regard for the customer comes in one of two forms. First, there are those businesses that provide services that are hard for us to understand, and we do not feel qualified to question the person providing the service. This is the case with health care providers and doctors, and it could also be true with other services ranging from college teaching to auto repair. The second type of business that may operate with little regard for the customer is a business that is "the only game in town." If you have ever driven across the desert and seen a lone gas station in the middle of nowhere, you will usually find high gas prices, dirty bathrooms, and a very rude cashier. If your tank is near empty and the next town is 2 hours down the road, you will eagerly pay double the price for a gallon of gas, reluctantly use the facilities, and put up with the cashier. Businesses that have a monopoly on providing a particular product or service may be able to stay in business precisely because they are the only one providing that product or service. Monopoly businesses should be careful, though, because sooner or later, an alternative business will set up shop and give customers another option.

The good news is that most businesses that ignore the customer do not stay in business over the long term, whether they are monopolies or whether they provide "sophisticated" services that the customer needs but doesn't understand. In either case, disgruntled customers spread bad news. Pretty soon, enough word gets around and customers make sure they have enough gas to make it to the next town, so they don't have to stop at the station that gouges prices and doesn't clean the restroom. Eventually, another gas station may go into business 20 miles down the road, giving travelers another option. Monopolies don't last forever if they ignore the customer. Even businesses that provide confusing and sophisticated services can't continue to ignore the customer. Disgruntled customers may be so upset with their primary care physician that they take the time to find out about health plans that allow them more than 5 minutes with a doctor.

Most customers are unpredictable in some ways but quite predictable in others. Disgruntled customers are very predictable in that they are unhappy, and when anyone is unhappy, they look for other people to talk to so that they can tell them all about their unhappiness. You can count on Disgruntled customers telling other people about the problems they had with the business that ignored their needs, that did not meet their expectations, or that did not provide the value they were looking for.

THE GOAL

If you were to take an assessment of your current customers, how would you classify them? Fill out the right hand column of Table 7.1, as you think about the external customers that you influence or serve directly.

Ideally you want 100% Loyal customers and 0% Disgruntled customers. However, it is unrealistic to think that 100% of your customers will fall in the Loyal category since it is impossible to please all of the people all of the time. So, how should your completed Table 7.1

 Table 7.1

CUSTOMER TYPE	PERCENT OF TOTAL CUSTOMER BASE
Loyal Customer	
Intrigued Customer	
Status Quo Customer	
Disgruntled Customer	
TOTAL PERCENT	100%

look? Is there an ideal mix of Customer Types to strive for? Once again, the 80/20 rule is a helpful guide to follow, when setting customer service goals:

- At least 80% of your customers should fall within the Loyal category.
- 20% or less of your customers will be, at any point in time, Intrigued, Status Quo, or Disgruntled customers.
- Of the 20% that are Intrigued, Status Quo, or Disgruntled, 80% should be in the Intrigued category—giving you a chance to convert them to Loyal customers in the near future.
- Status Quo and Disgruntled customers should be the lowest percentage of your business. Of the 20% that are Intrigued, Status Quo, or Disgruntled, no more than 10% should be in the Status Quo category.
- Of the 20% that are Intrigued, Status Quo, or Disgruntled, less than 10% should be in the Disgruntled category. This means that for every 100 customers, you should be dealing with no more than two customers who are Disgruntled.

The last guideline is extremely important. Let us say you operate a relatively small business, with 100 customers. Of those 100 customers, say that 10 of them are Disgruntled customers. Ten Disgruntled customers out of 100 total customers is a very dangerous situation because it can lead to widespread negative publicity and bad word of mouth about your company. Even 5 Disgruntled customers may outweigh the positive message that 20 Loyal and Intrigued customers may spread. The negative effect of 10 Disgruntled customers is more pronounced. This is because people are more motivated to talk to other people when they are upset. You can count on Disgruntled customers spreading negative messages about your business.

It is unavoidable that some customers are going to get upset, for one reason or another. Your goal is to make sure that those upset customers number 2 or less out of every 100 customers. You must also work to help Disgruntled customers solve their problems to the extent that they will not talk poorly of your business—even if they never come back. In other words, really listen to your Disgruntled customers and try to help them one last time. It is always better if a Disgruntled customer leaves a little less disgruntled since that reduces his motivation to talk negatively about your product or service. And who knows, once the customer's emotional reaction subsides and he has experienced other services, he may actually return one day after realizing that the grass is not always greener on the other service provider's side of the fence.

The percentages you identified can help you assess how your customers view you. Small businesses or business that operate in small industries must take extra care to identify their customers by type and manage them appropriately. Customers who buy products and services in these environments know each other well and are able to spread both good and bad news very quickly.

Whether you are a large multinational company or a small, nonprofit establishment, the ideal goal is always 100% customer satisfaction. The customer profile exercise balances that idealism with the reality of discriminating and high-maintenance customers. You will never be able to satisfy every customer in such a way that they become Loyal or Intrigued, but as a member of your organization you should never stop trying. In the end, some customers are hard to please and will remain Status Quo. Others, no matter what you do, will be Disgruntled customers, perhaps because of something you did, perhaps because of something totally unrelated to how you treated them. Still, we must do everything we can to reduce the number of Disgruntled customers to as close to zero as possible.

 Service summary for chapter 7

- ◆ Customers form expectations because they have needs;

- ◆ You do not automatically create customer satisfaction just because you meet a customer's expectations;

- ◆ Customer expectations are constantly changing and constantly increasing;

- ◆ If you can create or surface a need for a customer, and then fulfill it, you will create a Loyal customer;

- ◆ Know your Disgruntled customers, manage them best you can, and do all you can to make reparations; this will help avoid the negative word of mouth they might otherwise spread;

- ◆ Work toward the ideal of making every customer a Loyal customer—manage reality, however, as your customers will be a mix of Loyal, Intrigued, Status Quo, and Disgruntled customers. Use the 80/20 rule to help you achieve the right customer mix.

CHAPTER 8

PUTTING IT ALL TOGETHER

The seven ServiceElements are really a collection of tools to help every person, at every level of every organization deliver excellent customer service. We all know the characteristics of good customer service (ServiceElement #1), but a conscious and periodic review of those characteristics ensures that we will put them into practice. Excellent customer service also depends on how well we know and serve the external customer (ServiceElement #2).

When people think of customer service, they often think about a person who works behind a counter. They mistakenly think that it is only the person behind the counter who serves the customer, when the reality is that everyone plays a role when it comes to serving customers. That is why the notion of the internal customer is so important. Even if you only have contact with people who work with you, your actions eventually influence those who do have contact with the external customer.

Indeed, the critical role of internal customer service (ServiceElements #3) is often overlooked. Internal customer service is every bit as important as external customer service, with some arguing it is even more important. Coworkers and managers who work well together and treat each other like customers are far more likely to work in organizations that deliver excellent external customer service. That is because they foster a service oriented culture. Strong internal customer service naturally leads to strong external customer service.

Customer service is really about human dynamics and communication and thus goes far beyond the technical aspects of your product or service offerings. You cannot survive for long even if your product or service is the most unique and innovative offering on the market. In our world of globalization, technology, and international competitiveness, it becomes harder and harder to focus on technical product and service features if you wish to stand out. Competitors quickly copy whatever technical features might distinguish your product or service offering. The real differentiator is people, because it is not easy to replace people who understand and deliver excellent customer service on a consistent basis (ServiceElements #4). To deliver a total customer experience, every employee at every level must make their time count, in a way that improves customer service (ServiceElements #5). It is only then that we become sensitive to those critical Moments of Truth (ServiceElements #6) that most influence the customer experience.

The first six ServiceElements give you the tools to deliver excellent customer service. You are then in a position to create true satisfaction by not only meeting expectations but exceeding them (ServiceElement #7), transforming every internal and external customer into a Loyal Customer.

The ideas and theories behind all seven ServiceElements, are common sense and intuitive, but there are two common maladies that hinder us from putting this knowledge into practice:

Malady #1

Companies and the people within them know the things they should be doing, but they do not do them on a consistent basis.

Even worse,

Malady #2

Companies and the people within them know the things they should not be doing, but they continue to do them on a consistent basis.

Success is guaranteed for those people and companies who avoid these maladies and practice the seven ServiceElements. It takes a certain level of commitment to preach and practice the ServiceElements. An individual and leadership commitment to the ServiceElements will lead to service success across any organization's culture, because each ServiceElement is based on universal principles that underlie how we all think and act, or how we want others to treat us. These universal principles apply to rich and poor, supermarket shopper or airline passenger.

The bridge between knowing what we should be doing and actually doing it requires the creation of a culture—or more accurately a service culture. Companies and the

Figure 8.1

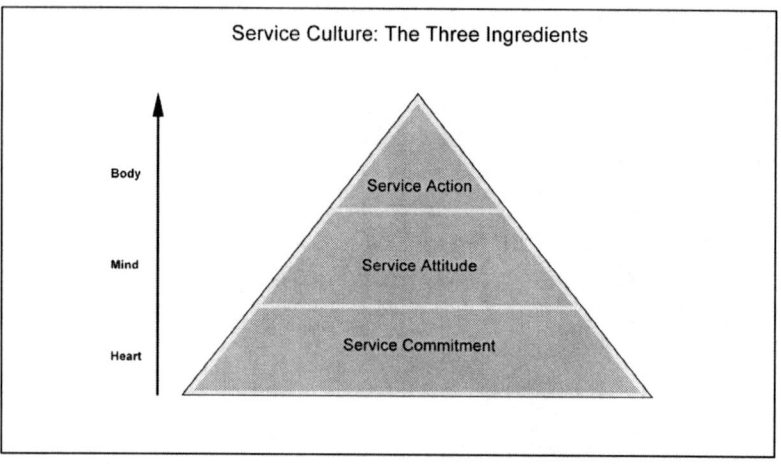

people who work within them can create a service culture by nurturing and growing three critical ingredients: commitment, attitude, and action. The presence of these three ingredients provides an environment in which the practice of the seven ServiceElements is accepted, encouraged, and quickly becomes the norm. Commitment, attitude, and action are all required, as shown in Figure 8.1. The heart, mind, and body all correspond to the different ingredients, as the figure also shows.

SERVICE COMMITMENT

People who are committed to service excellence know why their jobs are important. They know their work has meaning. They know that they are providing something to the customer, something that is important and meaningful. If you feel like you are giving something of value, then you will also find value in how you provide it. We were once asked to speak at a yearly employee meeting for a large Las Vegas hotel. Our job was to motivate the employees and let them know that teamwork was important to the overall success of the hotel. Employees came from every corner of the hotel for the event. The cooks had on their chef's hats, the cocktail waitresses were in their outfits, poker dealers had on their uniforms, and human resources and other professional staff were in business attire. It was quite a mixture of folks. Prior to the formal start of the event, I (Mario) was visiting with a few of the chefs. I asked one of the chefs *why* he liked his job. His enthusiasm was contagious. He said he liked his job because he "made creations" that satisfy people and make them happy! There is someone who understands the meaning of his job. His job certainly involves cooking meats, roasting vegetables, and making wonderful sauces, but the end result is satisfaction and happiness. In fact, every employee in the Las Vegas hotel contributes to or takes away from the entertainment of every customer who walks through the door. The top employees at the Las Vegas hotel understand that they deliver an entertainment experience (whether that be found in food or activity), and that is what defines excellent customer service in this industry.

If you understand what it is that you deliver and why it is important, you will feel your job makes a difference. That is why commitment is associated with the heart. A heartfelt commitment to your job means that you will do your job with enthusiasm and deliver excellent customer service because you believe in what you do. Commitment is the foundation to building a service culture. Without commitment, there is no emotional connection to sustain us. You may convince yourself logically that your job is important, but until you feel it, you will never be truly motivated. Think about the companies that you associate with excellent customer service. The simple fact is that organizations and people that deliver excellent customer service are passionate about their jobs because they believe in what they do, deep down in their hearts. Indeed, it is the heartfelt commitment that forms the foundation of any service culture. A leader may mandate that employees attend training or make changes, but if this same leader does not work to gain commitment and touch hearts, then there will be no change in culture.

How, then, do you as an individual begin to build commitment? The series of statements and questions below will help you, your department, or entire organization open the dialogue that is needed to start building the commitment ingredient:

- ✓ Read the mission of your organization.
    - What do you think the mission means?

- ✓ Does your organization have values printed or listed anywhere? If not, there is a problem. If the values are printed somewhere, read them.
    - What do these values mean to you, as it relates to you personally and to your job?

- ✓ Now that you have read the mission and values of the organization think about your job.
    - Why is your job important?
    - What are you providing to customers, as you do your job on a daily basis?

- ✓ How do you influence internal and external customer service?

✓ Are you influencing internal and external customers positively or negatively?

Many people in seminars and workshops look at their company's vision, mission, or values and become discouraged. They see words like integrity, responsibility, excellence, and passion but feel that these values are not practiced every day in the organization, or by *certain* people.

The mission, values, and goals of an organization are the ideals that you and everyone in the organization should strive for. That does not mean that every interaction and every situation will perfectly exemplify these ideal values. People make mistakes, including chief executives, managers, and coworkers. Sometimes we react to a difficult customer inappropriately. The mission, values, and goals remain important, though, because they help connect us to the things we should be thinking about, as individuals. Don't spend your time worrying about whether other people are working toward the mission, living the values, or achieving the goals. If you believe in the ideals that are embodied in these things, then you will find it incredibly easy to see why your job matters. This will make it easy for you to commit to excellent customer service. You will feel invigorated and fulfilled by serving others. Above all, do not worry about the commitment of others, simply work to deepen your own.

SERVICE ATTITUDE

When you believe in what you do, it isn't very hard to motivate yourself to do what you need to do. That is because you want to do it! A strong commitment fuels a strong service attitude. Attitudes are individually determined. As basic as it sounds, if you are mentally determined to change your attitude, it will change. This is why Figure 8.1 shows that your attitude is associated with your mind.

The psychology of the mind is a critical factor in determining not only attitude but individual happiness and overall health. A whole new field in psychology is now studying happiness. What Dr. Martin Seligman and other pioneers in the field have found is that positive, conscious choices lead to happy and healthful lives. In the 1970s, a man named Norman Cousins became famous after he decided the antidote for a debilitating illness was 6 months of laughter therapy. Cousins watched funny movies and television shows, such as the Three Stooges, over and over again during a 6 month period, and to the doctors' amazement they found his disease had somehow disappeared. Apparently his positive attitude had stimulated body-curing endorphins that played a role in his recovery. If we choose to focus on the positive and the powerful, we will have a powerful service attitude to match our powerful service commitment. But, like Norman Cousins, we must make the choice to adopt a positive attitude. We may not cure diseases, but we will solve customer problems and help build a progressive service culture in our businesses and organizations.

Admittedly, there are many things in an organization that are beyond your control. If you focus on those things you do not control, then your attitude will slowly deteriorate, even if you started off with a deep commitment to your organization. In virtually every industry across the globe, corporate buyouts and mergers leave scores of employees guessing about what the new owners might demand, or what departments might merge or separate. Buyouts and mergers are part of corporate life today, and changes are certain when such events occur.

Through all of this, the key to a positive attitude remains: focus on those things that you can control. Sales author and speaker Jeffrey Gitomer says you should resign your position as general manager of the universe. In other words, don't worry about things that you cannot affect. Instead, focus on those things you can influence, like the quality of your effort at work, or the way you treat internal and external customers.

Many people feel that motivational speakers and books are overly optimistic. In a sense, it is true that everyone has bad days. There are times when you simply do not feel upbeat and motivated, so your attitude suffers. But psychologist Paul Ekman's research offers some hope, even on those days when things are not going so well. If you are not feeling very motivated and are suffering from a bad attitude, change from the outside in. Normally, we think that our facial expression and body posture are reflections of how we feel on the inside. When we are sad or upset, our shoulders slump and mouths turn downward. Dr. Ekman suggests that changing your facial expression from a frown to a smile actually changes your body chemistry (the inside) and thus gives you a fighting chance to change your attitude. Dr. Ekman gives us all hope, because attitude is determined in your own mind: if you believe it, you will feel it. The following 10 points will help you develop or maintain a positive attitude and contribute to a powerful service culture:

- ✓ Smile at people and make eye contact with others;

- ✓ Make humor and laughing a part of your life;

- ✓ If you are on the phone, make sure your voice, body posture, and facial expressions all reflect a positive attitude just as if you were talking face-to-face with a customer;

✓ Praise people and thank them for small things;

✓ Call your internal and external customers by name;

✓ Remember that what counts most in life is what we do for others;

✓ Make an effort to listen to or read positive material;

✓ If you have to resolve a disagreement with a coworker, be the one to initiate a solution even if you feel the start of the problem wasn't your fault;

✓ At the start of every day, choose a positive attitude;

✓ Before every conversation or correspondence with a customer, choose a positive attitude.

You determine your attitude. Rhonda Byrne, who wrote the phenomenally popular book *The Secret*, puts it this way: Your life is a mirror of the dominant thoughts you think. Human beings can use their free will to choose their thoughts. Byrne's insight is good news for you. You can choose your attitude.

SERVICE ACTION

Service Question: What do you call a person who is committed to a cause and has a great attitude but never gets around to taking the action to make things happen?

(a) Unemployed
(b) A philosopher
(c) A procrastinator
(d) All or any of the above

The answer to the Service Question is "D. All or any of the above." We have all met people with big dreams and plans. They are sold on the vision of a better life for themselves and others. They are infinitely positive, and just talking to them gets you excited. These are the people who want to start their own business, strive for the big promotion, or start buying up houses to rent so that they can become real estate moguls. They are emotionally committed and have that positive mental attitude. There is only one problem. Their hopes and dreams remain hopes and dreams because they never take any steps to move toward those hopes and dreams. There is no action. These are the people who are philosophers because they have all the answers and can tell us what to do even though they have not shown us that they can do it themselves. These are the people who have big plans—and they assure us that they will start tomorrow or next week, even though tomorrow or next week never seems to come. When you have all the answers but never do anything yourself, you are an unemployed philosopher with a bad reputation for procrastinating. Not a very flattering description.

Action is associated with activity, with doing. We sometimes hear participants in our seminars and workshops say, "We know all about customer service, so how is this going to help me?" We usually respond by presenting them with the two Maladies that we showed at the beginning of the chapter. We then confirm that we know that they know this information, but we ask them "If you know it, do you consistently do it? Do you have the tools and the psychological mindset and commitment to take the action?"

You need your body and mind to engage in activity if you are to move toward your commitments with the proper attitude. This book has provided application tools and exercises that are associated with every Service-Element. If you have completed these tools and exercises, then you have already taken the action to deliver excellent customer service and contribute to a culture that can sustain it. The tools and exercises also serve as common sense reminders for you to keep on doing the things you should be doing and avoid doing the things you know you shouldn't be doing.

Many people have trouble committing to the mission and goals of their organization, even though they are "doers" who do not like to sit still. They like to take action and stay busy, but it is hard to have the right attitude when you feel like coworkers are not pulling their own weight or they are not as excited or committed as you. The problem becomes even more acute when you see others cutting corners, cheating the system, or taking credit for someone else's work. If you are caught in any situation of this sort, you must in fact remember that the only person you control is you.

The key to cultivating all three service culture ingredients may be somewhat opposite to what we have described up to this point if you are an action-oriented person. First, take the necessary action to help your organization fulfill its goals and objectives. Continue to take actions that help the team and organization, even if your current motivation is not fueled by a belief in the mission and goals of the organization. Next, while you are taking those actions, make observations along the way. Notice how internal customers respond to someone who is always willing to help, without complaint or expectation of payback. Notice how a focus on service makes your external customers feel. Finally, ask people if you have helped them. Ask them how you can help them. Ask them if you can do more.

If you are an action person and you focus on the results of your actions—how they make others feel—you will invariably find that others find meaning in your actions. When others find meaning in your actions, you can't help but discover that your actions *are* meaningful and purposeful. You will be motivated to continue your actions, because you will quickly realize that the highest form of service is providing something of value to another person. You will discover that most organizational missions and values strive to realize the ideals that we all believe in. Believe in these ideals and do everything within your power to become a servant of others. Find joy in service. You just may be the person responsible for starting a true customer service culture in your organization!

ABOUT THE AUTHORS

Mario Martinez, PhD, is an associate professor of higher education at the University of Nevada, Las Vegas, and executive for ServiceElements International. He has worked as a professional speaker since 1997 delivering keynote speeches and seminars on issues related to human and organizational dynamics. Mario's previous book topics range from empowerment to demography as it pertains to the demand for higher education.

Bob Hobbi is the founder, president, and CEO of ServiceElements. He has more than 25 years of experience in providing industry-leading solutions in customer service, strategic excellence training, coaching and consultative services, and business development. Bob served in various executive positions in the aviation industry prior to founding ServiceElements. He is a member of various business associations and contributes to several charity and community organizations.

LaVergne, TN USA
15 December 2009

167044LV00007B/1/P